A HANDBOOK

OF

MODAL COUNTERPOINT

A Handbook of Modal Counterpoint

Stella Roberts
and
Irwin Fischer

New York, THE FREE PRESS COLLIER-MACMILLAN LIMITED, *London*

Preface

In our day, among both performers and scholars, a growing appreciation of the music of the Renaissance has laid upon the theory teacher the happy task of providing studies based upon that literature—studies now considered fully as essential to the education of the music student as those of eighteenth- and nineteenth-century masterworks.

It is the technical foundation of the sixteenth-century style that the authors of this Handbook have undertaken to present in a form explicit enough for a first approach to the subject. To lay this foundation, they have adopted the time-honored method of the Cantus Firmus and Five Species. True, the Cantus Firmus was no longer in general use in sixteenth-century composition; but it was still the basis of the method by which those composers learned their craft, and it must have shaped their thought as well as their technique. In retracing the steps of those learners, the present-day student may come to share that thought, to sense the spirit behind the tangible elements of the style.

In the treatises of the era that also served as textbooks the Cantus Firmus is a feature in common. Some of the cantus, selected from works of Zarlino and Morley, arc used in shortened form in this book. In a few of the treatises published toward the end of the era, the Five Species appear and several more besides, obviously devised for pedagogical utility. What could be more sensible than to attack one rhythmic problem at a time?

The primary purpose of the Species system should be clearly understood: It is to establish the relation between consonance, dissonance, and accent, the *harmonic* foundation of the technique. Underlying a melodic rhythm that is wonderfully free and flexible, is a harmonic rhythm that is metric and steady, well represented in the Species. When these are mastered, the Cantus Firmus may be discarded and free composition may begin, to become stylistically complete with all the resources of melodic design, contrapuntal devices, form, and idiom.

Because it is practical in many ways, the authors have introduced the complete clef system, and have made the use of alto and tenor C clefs a requirement, since they are in present-day use by orchestral instruments. Every student should learn to read these two clefs, and those who look forward to intensive studies in theory or musicology should work with the others also.

Again as a practical and indispensable aid, the authors recommend the use of Arabic numerals for analysis of intervals above the bass. In three- and four-part counterpoint they have added a nonfunctional chordal analysis, in which triads and seventh chords are indicated by symbols that show root and structure. Thus, by the use of modern unit-names, the student easily learns to recognize the familiar harmonies that the sixteenth-century theorist was obliged to laboriously describe as several sets of intervals.

The benefit to the student of a course such as this is often a delayed-action effect, more apparent in the following years than during the course itself. Among the authors' own students many have reported improved aural imagination, a better ability to hear harmonies in the mind's ear. Some students, having become acquainted with a style based principally on the works of the conservative Palestrina, have been struck by the held-over features as well as the new ones in the progressive secular works of the era, and even in the practices of later eras—a wholesome observation for modern-minded young persons. Most students have easily grasped the figured-bass concept of Baroque harmony, having seen it grow under their pencils. Almost all have been able to recognize modal effects in folk song and in art works of the nineteenth and twentieth centuries.

To the serious student who seeks a complete exposition of the Renaissance style, the authors recommend the following works, noted for their brilliant scholarship, and the source of much of the stylistic content of this book:

Jeppesen, Knud. *The Style of Palestrina and the Dissonance*, trans. by Margaret Hamerik (London: Humphrey Milford, Oxford University Press, 1927).
———. *Counterpoint*, trans. by Glen Haydon (Englewood Cliffs, N.J.: Prentice-Hall, 1939).
Merritt, Arthur T. *Sixteenth-Century Polyphony* (Cambridge, Mass.: Harvard University Press, 1944).
Morris, R. O. *Contrapuntal Technique in the Sixteenth Century* (Oxford at the Clarendon Press, 1922).
Soderlund, Gustave, F. *Direct Approach to Counterpoint in the 16th Century Style* (Appleton-Century-Crofts, 1947).

The authors hope that their book will be found adaptable to the requirements of various curricula, and at any of several levels, with only the prerequisite of a first-year course in harmony. That such studies should be introduced somewhere in the curriculum seems imperative, for they form a vital link in musical understanding.   S.R.
                                                                                      I.F.

Chicago, Illinois

Contents

CHAPTER 1

Introduction

Since most students who embark upon a course in Counterpoint will have studied at least a year of Harmony, a comparison of the two branches of musical study may be in order.

1. Harmony deals with chords in succession, Counterpoint with melodies in combination.

2. Harmony is expressed in the vertical aspect of the written score; in Counterpoint the emphasis is on the horizontal aspect.

3. Harmony may be said to concern itself chiefly with the element of color in music; Counterpoint is concerned more with line.

4. In Harmony one melody is likely to predominate; in Counterpoint all parts should be of almost equal melodic interest.

5. In Harmony all parts unite to convey a single idea; in Counterpoint each part conveys its distinct and individual idea.

Points 4 and 5 above explain the essential difference between music that is homophonic (of the later harmonic period) and that which is polyphonic (of the preceding contrapuntal period). It is true, however, that many works of the best composers of both periods resemble each other, so that we may justly feel that Harmony and Counterpoint are really two different views of the same thing. Knud Jeppesen has written, "The best results of contrapuntal and of harmonic instruction are . . . in the last analysis, almost identical" (*Counterpoint*, p. 4).

Nevertheless, clear and unequivocal examples of the two styles are not hard to find. The homophonic (many-voices-blended-into-one) style is exemplified by a melody with accompaniment or by a simple hymn; the polyphonic (many-voiced) style by a fugue or a movement from a 16th-century mass; a third, the monophonic (one-voiced) style, is to be found in its most sustained form in Gregorian Chant.

In the study of Harmony, the Bach-to-Brahms period is usually chosen as the historical point of reference, because that is the period in which the most advanced harmonic resources were developed.

In Counterpoint, however, there are two great eras that must be studied. Most musicians are quite well acquainted with the Baroque period through the music of Bach, its greatest representative, whose style is tonal, instrumental, and harmonically sophisticated. With the Renaissance period there is unfortunately less familiarity, though the name of its greatest composer, Palestrina, is well known. His style is harmonically transparent and simple, his music is all for voices *a capella*, and its basis is not the familiar major-minor tonal system but that which immediately preceded it, the system of the polyphonic modes. A good musician must be acquainted with both styles.

We have chosen the late Renaissance, the 16th century, as the style-period for a first course, partly because the technique is simpler, partly because the style of the Baroque is built on it as foundation.

To pursue the study of the Renaissance style, we shall follow four procedures not commonly used in courses in Harmony.

1. The use of the C clefs and open score.

2. The use of the polyphonic modes as a scale basis.

3. The use of a given melody, known as a Cantus Firmus, against which—above or below or both—are written other melodies or voices, often spoken of as counterpoints.

4. The study of one rhythmic problem at a time in a traditional system of five species, or orders, which will be taken up as follows:

First Species: Note against note.
Second Species: Two notes against each one of the Cantus Firmus.
Third Species: Four notes against one.
Fourth Species: Syncopation, or tied-over half notes.
Fifth Species: Florid style, using varied time values.

This species system has been the basis of teaching Counterpoint for generations, and though there have been attempts to find other methods, none more satisfactory has been found.

The first of these procedures, use of the C clefs, will be the subject of the first lesson. The second lesson will be devoted to the modes, the third lesson to two-part counterpoint in First Species.

A word of admonition! In no course are work-methods so important. The student should follow directions closely and be content to move step by step. He should not try to do a whole assignment at one study session.

The C Clefs

Three clef signs are used in our system of notation:

Example 1

1. The C clef sign, which locates Middle C:

2. The G clef sign, which locates G above Middle C:

3. The F clef sign, which locates F below Middle C:

The Great Staff of eleven lines shows the relative positions of all the clefs, including those no longer in general use:

Example 2

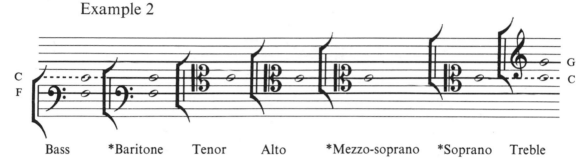

Bass *Baritone Tenor Alto *Mezzo-soprano *Soprano Treble

The clefs marked with an asterisk (*) are obsolete today, except as they are used for transposition. The alto and tenor clefs, however, are still in use for orchestral instruments, the former for viola and alto trombone, the latter for cello, bassoon, and tenor trombone.

Note that Middle C is always on a line, and may be placed on any line in the complete clef system:

Example 3

Bass *Baritone Tenor Alto *Mezzo-soprano *Soprano Treble

Another diagram of the four clefs we shall use, and their relationships to each other, may be helpful:

Example 4

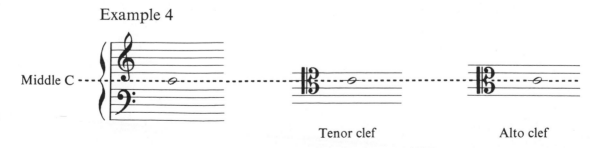

Middle C ········

Tenor clef Alto clef

Although the student will not use the following signatures in this course, he should know the proper positions of the sharps and flats in the C clefs:

Example 5

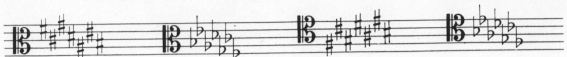

Assignment I

Exercise 1

Write the following melodies in either alto or tenor clef, whichever is appropriate:

Exercise 2

Write the following melodies in bass or treble clef, whichever is appropriate:

The Modes

The value of knowing the modes is not only for their historical importance. Many contemporary composers have used modal effects—Vaughan Williams, Ravel, and Bartok, to name only a few, as well as Beethoven, Chopin, and Brahms among the older composers.

The system of modes was devised to classify the great body of melodies that were the monophonic chants of the medieval Christian Church.

Within modal usage there are two distinct practices, as different from each other as either of them is from our major-minor system. These are:

1. The Gregorian system, which prevailed approximately from early medieval times through the twelfth century.

2. The polyphonic system, which flourished during the fifteenth and sixteenth centuries.

THE GREGORIAN MODES

Although classification of modal melodies in relation to a well-organized system of scales was not accomplished until the late eighth century, or possibly even later, Pope Gregory the Great (590–604), is credited with efforts toward the organization of the melodies used by the Roman Catholic Church. Hence the frequent designation of this system of classification as the Gregorian Modes, and of the chants themselves and the style of performing them as Gregorian Chant. Since these modes remain the basis of classification through the Middle Ages, they are often called the Medieval or Ecclesiastical Modes.

1. The naming of the scales in the Gregorian system was derived from the complex system of the Classical Greeks.

2. The Gregorian scales have the same names as the Greek, but the names are applied to different scales, owing possibly to errors or misunderstandings in medieval scholarship.

3. The system uses what we think of as white keys, plus one accidental, B♭. No sharps were used. Each mode is a different octave segment of the "white-key" series.

4. Two tones in each mode are more important than the others. These are:
   a. The Final, or concluding tone, marked F in Example 6.
   b. The Dominant, the tone on which a noticeably greater number of syllables are sung, marked D in Example 6.

5. Gregorian modes are divided into two classes according to the position of the Final in relation to the range of the scale-melody. When the range of a melody lies mostly between the low Final and that an octave higher, the melody is in an authentic mode. When the range of a melody lies from a fourth below the Final to a fifth above it, the melody is in a plagal mode. Thus one authentic and one plagal mode share each Final, as shown in Example 6.

6. The Dominant is a *tone*, not a chord. It is the reciting tone, a tone of suspense or tension, and the Final is the tone of repose. In this respect their function is not unlike our harmonic dominant and tonic. The position of the Gregorian Dominant, however, was not as stable as ours.
   a. In the authentic modes it is the fifth above the Final, except in mode iii, the Phrygian, where B is replaced by C. (Since B was a variable tone, B or B♭, it was not considered suitable for the important function of Dominant.)
   b. In the plagal modes it is a 3rd below the dominant of the companion authentic mode, except that here also B is replaced by C.

7. Certain characteristic patterns and cadences belong to each mode, as well as an idiomatic tendency to emphasize certain tones and suppress others.

8. In general, Gregorian melody lacks leading tone effects.

The four authentic and four plagal Gregorian modes, with their names, numbers, Finals and Dominants, are shown in Example 6.

Example 6

Authentic Modes

Plagal Modes

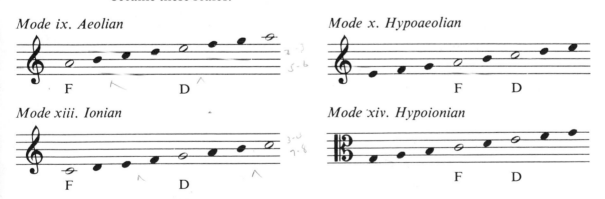

Mode i. Dorian

Mode ii. Hypodorian

Mode iii. Phrygian

Mode iv. Hypophrygian

Mode v. Lydian

Mode vi. Hypolydian

Mode vii. Mixolydian

Mode viii. Hypomixolydian

Two other modes, classified by medieval theorists as Secular, are also shown. Their resemblance to our A minor and C major scales is obvious; eventually they became these scales.

Mode ix. Aeolian

Mode x. Hypoaeolian

Mode xiii. Ionian

Mode xiv. Hypoionian

Numbers xi and xii, not included in the above table, refer to the Locrian and Hypolocrian modes; these are theoretical modes not used in the Gregorian system.

THE POLYPHONIC MODES

As the monophony of the Middle Ages developed through organum and discant into the polyphony of the Renaissance, harmonic resources and concepts grew, and the modes gradually changed, so that by the time of Palestrina a new system had evolved to meet the requirements of the newer harmonic music. The polyphonic modes were the intermediate forms between the Gregorian modes and our major-minor system. Here are the significant changes:

1. Plagal and authentic distinctions become unimportant, since some voices in a score of the newer polyphonic music must, of necessity, be in the authentic range, others in the plagal, throughout the work.

2. The two modes, Aeolian and Ionian, rejected by the Gregorian theorists for church use, are now admitted to use in sacred music.

3. The Dominant becomes a *chord* of activity and suspense, with a strong tendency to move to a point of rest. It is always the fifth degree of the mode, even when that degree is B.

4. The preference for major triads on both Dominant and Final brought about alterations upward, or sharps.

    a. The major triad on the Dominant introduces the leading tone, but at cadences only:

        F♯ in the Mixolydian,

        C♯ in the Dorian,

        G♯ in the Aeolian.

    But *not* D♯ in the Phrygian; here the leading tone is F at the lower end of the scale.

    b. The major triad on the Final introduces the Tierce de Picardie:

        F♯ in the Dorian,

        C♯ in the Aeolian,

        G♯ in the Phrygian.

5. B♭ is often used descending to A, or in relation to F. The Lydian mode practically disappears because of this practice, since it becomes the transposed Ionian. Should B occur in a Lydian or Dorian cadence, it must be altered to B♭.

6. One transposition was used, and one only—that with one flat in the signature. Here E♭ takes the place of B♭ in the untransposed modes. The keyboard of the Renaissance was then tuned and "spelled":

Example 7

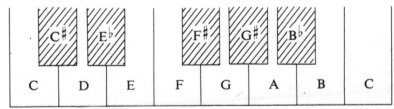

7. Cadences sound, in modern terms, like V, V6, or vii$_6^0$ to I in major; and in the Phrygian mode, like iv, iv$_6$, or ii$_6^0$ to V in minor. In free writing—that is, writing without Cantus Firmus—IV to I is also used.

8. There is no modulation in the modern sense. The mode of a composition, no matter how long, remains the same throughout. Variety is provided, however, by cadences on other degrees than the Final.

9. A modal melody may begin on almost any degree of the mode. Endings, however, are on the Final.

The polyphonic modes are shown in Example 8.

Example 8

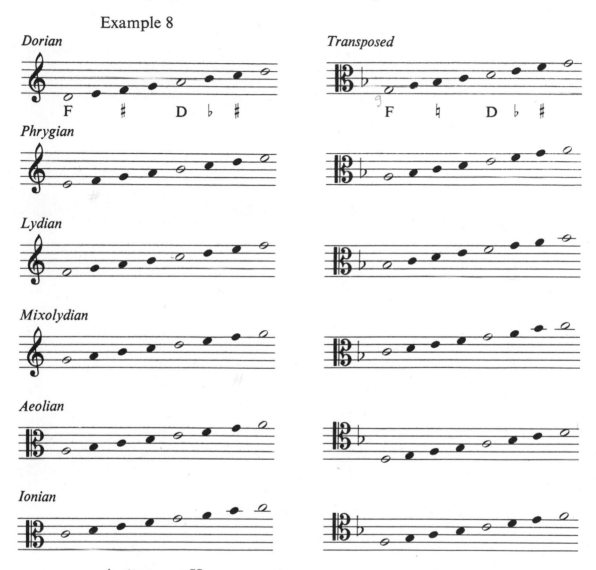

Assignment II

Exercise 1

Write out the six polyphonic modes in their untransposed and transposed forms, showing the accidentals which may be used in each, and also their Finals and Dominants, as illustrated in the Dorian mode in Example 8.

Exercise 2

Read the following pages on First Species counterpoint in two parts, pages 11 through 17.

Two-Part Counterpoint

First Species in Two Parts

MELODIC PRINCIPLES

1. In First Species, or note-against-note counterpoint, both conjunct (stepwise) and disjunct (leaping) motion may be used, but conjunct motion should predominate.

2. The melodic intervals available are:

Conjunctly: Major and minor 2nds. No augmented 2nds and no chromatic progressions may be used.

Disjunctly: Minor and major 3rds, perfect 4ths and 5ths, minor 6ths *ascending only*, and perfect octaves. Leaps of a major 6th are rare, and all kinds of 7ths, all diminished, augmented, and compound intervals are foreign to the style. (A compound interval is an interval larger than an octave.)

3. More than two consecutive skips in the same direction are poor.

4. The following intervals with one note intervening should not be used if the motion is continuous up or down:

    a. a major 7th

    b. any compound interval

    c. an augmented 4th, though its inversion, a diminished 5th, is good

    d. a minor 7th made of two perfect 4th leaps; but a perfect 5th followed by a minor 3rd is good ascending, particularly in the Dorian mode, but not descending.

Example 9

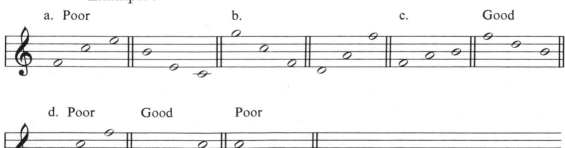

5. Leaps of an octave or of a minor 6th should be preceded and succeeded by notes within the leap.

Example 10

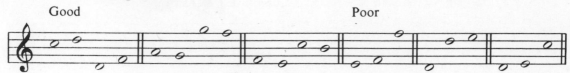

6. Occasional repeated or tied-over notes are allowed, but preferably not more than one in an exercise.

7. Monotony, resulting either from repetition of short melodic patterns or from lack of variety in range, is poor. A good melodic curve should be evident, with a high climactic point touched upon only once, and, if possible, also a lowest tone heard only once.

Example 11

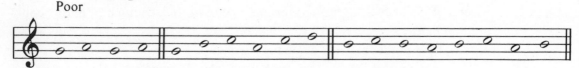

8. The following ranges of voices should be observed:

Example 12

9. Musica Ficta is the name given to the stylized use of accidentals in Renaissance modal writing. Those used for melodic reasons are as follows:

    a. The flatted B or, less frequently, the sharped F is often necessary to avoid the interval of an augmented 4th or diminished 5th by direct leap, or the augmented 4th in the extremes of a short melodic progression. In general, the accidental should be applied to the second of the two troublesome notes.

    b. B occurring between two A's is usually flatted, except in cases where so doing causes other undesirable consequences, possibly harmonic, as in relationship with E.

    c. B is often flatted in descending scalewise motion.

    d. F♯ may be used to avoid an augmented 2nd in approaching a cadence in the Aeolian mode.

    e. Transposition of the modes a 4th up or a 5th down, with a B♭ in the signature, requires the use of E♭ and B♮ in place of B♭ or F♯ respectively in the untransposed modes.

The too frequent or unnecessary use of these accidentals tends to destroy the individualities of the modes. Historically it led to their disappearance, or rather their dissolution into our major-minor system. Even during the Renaissance, the Lydian mode lost its character because of the constant use of B♭.

HARMONIC PRINCIPLES

1. First Species counterpoint consists of one whole note in the added voice against each whole note of the Cantus Firmus, abbreviated C. F.

2. The intervals between the two voices (harmonic intervals) must always be consonant. Consonances are either perfect or imperfect.

    a. The perfect consonances are the unison, the perfect 5th and the perfect octave.

    b. The imperfect consonances are minor and major 3rds, and minor and major 6ths.

    c. All other intervals, *including the perfect 4th*, are dissonances in two-part counterpoint.

3. The opening interval should be a perfect consonance:

    a. above the C. F., a perfect octave, 5th or unison

    b. below the C. F., a perfect octave or unison.

4. The unison should be used only in the first or last measure.

5. In general, imperfect consonances are preferable to perfect consonances.

6. Voices should generally not be more than a 12th apart, except in the interest of improving the melodic line.

7. More than three, or at most four, consecutive 3rds or 6ths in similar motion should be avoided.

8. Crossing of voices is common practice in contrapuntal writing. Even occasional overlapping, if the melody is improved, is not ruled out.

9. Parallel 5ths and octaves are prohibited because of lack of independence of the parts. However, consecutive 5ths are correct when they occur as follows:

    a. from crossed voices

    b. from contrary motion.

Example 13

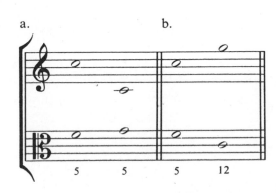

10. Similar motion from any interval to an octave, 5th or unison, called a direct or hidden octave, 5th or unison, should be avoided in two-part writing.

Example 14

11. The last two tones in the C. F. form the cadence, the word derived from the Latin *cadere*, "to fall". These two tones are a descent from the second degree to the Final in the C. F.

When the C. F. is in the lower voice the counterpoint forms a major 6th to an octave with these two tones. When the C. F. is in the upper voice the counterpoint forms a minor 3rd to a unison, or a minor 10th to an octave.

This requires the use of sharps (leading tones) in the Dorian, Mixolydian, and Aeolian modes, as shown in Example 15.

Example 15

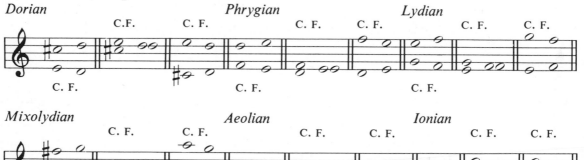

Example 16. FIRST SPECIES IN TWO PARTS—MODEL EXAMPLES

a. *Dorian*

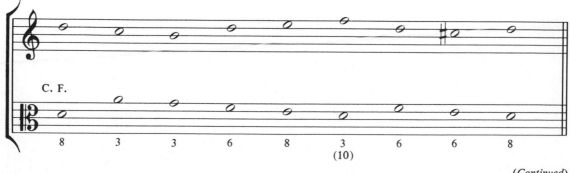

(10)

(*Continued*)

b. *Phrygian transposed*

c. *Mixolydian*

d. *Lydian*

e. *Aeolian*

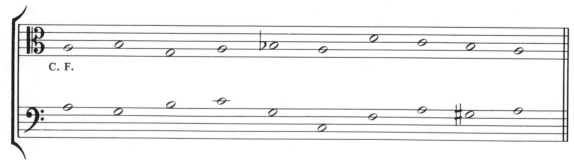

(*Continued*)

f. *Ionian transposed*

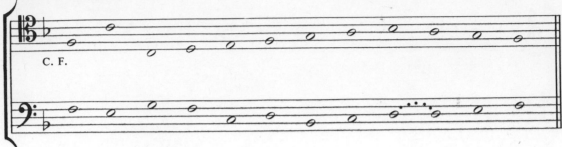

C. F.

Assignment III

Write a counterpoint in First Species above each of the following C. F.'s, using them in the given clefs. Use a different clef in the counterpoint from that in the C. F.

Dorian

Phrygian

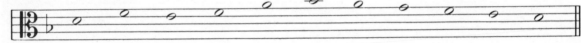

Aeolian transposed

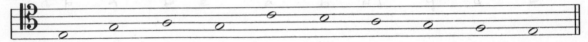

Assignment IV

Write a counterpoint in First Species below each of the following C. F.'s. Transpose at least one of them.

IMPORTANT—

1. The C. F. may be transposed up or down an octave, without change of signature, or up a 4th or down a 5th, with the signature of one flat. The purpose of the transposition is to place the C. F. in the range of a different voice. This requires an appropriate change of clef.

2. In this and all future assignments:

   a. Name the mode of each C. F.

   b. Use a separate staff and a different clef for each of the voices. The same clef should not be used for two of the voices in any exercise.

c. Use clefs in the natural order of voice ranges—soprano (treble clef) above alto, alto above tenor, tenor above bass.

d. Write in the analysis figures as shown in the first of the examples.

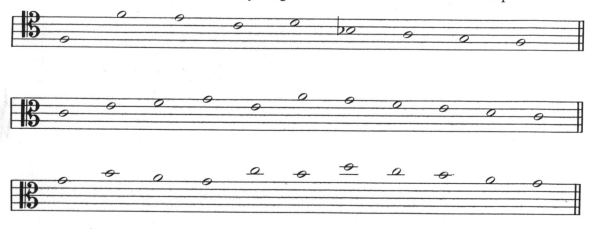

Second Species in Two Parts

METER AND RHYTHM

The difference between meter and rhythm is often not clearly understood, though it is an important one. On the other hand, this difference is easier to describe than to define. <u>Meter</u> has to do with the measuring of time values; <u>rhythm</u> is their organization into patterns. Meter is indicated by time signatures and fixes the limits of measures, while rhythm lies in the content of the measures.

For example, a waltz, a minuet, a saraband, a mazurka, and a polonaise are all in triple meter, usually indicated by a 3/4 time signature. But the rhythms of these dances are strikingly different from each other because of tempo, accentuation, and variety of note values.

In church music of the Renaissance the beat-unit is usually the half note, but occasionally the quarter note. In secular music the beat-unit is commonly the quarter note. In either case, writers of the period compare the movement of the beat to the normal pulse, which is the metronome rate of 72 to 80.

The same rhythmic content may look very different in the metric notations of different periods. Where the composer of the 16th century might have written the fragment shown in Example 17a, Bach wrote it as in Example 17b.

Example 17

a.

b.   *Jesu, Leiden, Pein und Tod*

In Example 18 another example of identical rhythms in different notations is shown.

Example 18

A study in Counterpoint

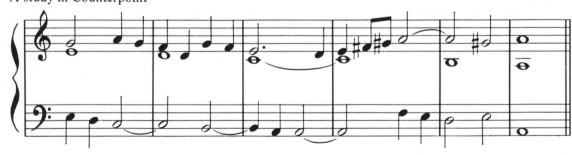

The same passage in "a capella" time (4/2)

(Continued)

The same passage in the metric notation of the late Baroque

In the studies in this book the half note is the beat-unit, and the C. F. represents two beats. Although no bar lines were used in 16th century music, it is convenient in early studies to use them, writing one note of the C. F. to the measure.

MELODIC PRINCIPLES

The usage outlined for First Species melody remains basically the same for Second Species, with some additions and exceptions necessary to maintain the half-note texture, which will consist of alternating strong and weak beats.

1. Immediately repeated half notes will not be used, nor will half notes be tied over, the latter forming the basis of Fourth Species.

2. To emphasize the rhythmic independence of the parts, the counterpoint should begin on a weak beat.

3. After scale steps, a leap in the same direction to an accented half note is awkward.

Example 19

4. The melodic interval of an augmented 4th or augmented 5th on successive strong beats should be avoided unless the melodic movement has changed direction. These intervals should also be avoided as the extreme high and low notes of a melodic passage.

Example 20

5. Repetition of melodic pattern, exact or in sequence, is not typical of Renaissance music.

6. Melodic interest, manifested in good use of available range, and in climactic high and low points, is vitally important.

HARMONIC PRINCIPLES

1. Second Species consists of two half notes against each whole note of the C. F. Those that fall with the C. F. notes will be strong beats, the others weak.

2. The strong half notes must always be consonant with the C. F., just as in First Species.

3. The weak beats may be either consonant or dissonant, but if dissonant, they must be passing tones, that is, approached and left by step.

4. Dissonant auxiliaries are not in the style, but the auxiliary figure may appear if only consonances are involved, 5th to 6th, or 6th to 5th.

Example 21

5. Unisons may be used on weak beats.

6. Perfect concords of the same size—unisons, 5ths, or octaves—are correct on weak beats of successive measures but incorrect on successive strong beats, or from a weak to the next strong beat. A 5th and a 12th, or the reverse, called 5ths in contrary motion, are correct on any beats of successive measures.

Example 22

7. Again, direct octaves and 5ths are to be avoided.

8. Opening intervals should be the same as those for First Species.

9. In analysis it is advisable to circle the figures that indicate dissonances, as shown in Examples 21 and 24.

10. The last two intervals between the C. F. and the counterpoint are the same as those given for First Species. If necessary, the penultimate measure (next to the last) may contain a whole note, as in First Species, since an octave leap from the leading tone is poor. But note, in the Phrygian mode the leading tone is F, not D; the octave leap from D is good.

11. Cadences are given in Example 23.

Example 23

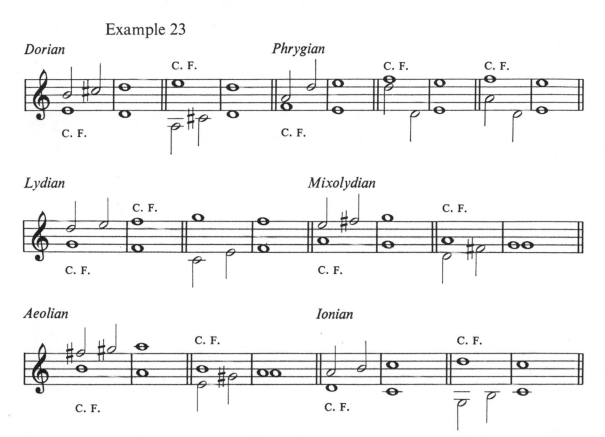

Example. 24. SECOND SPECIES IN TWO PARTS—MODEL EXAMPLES

a. *Lydian*

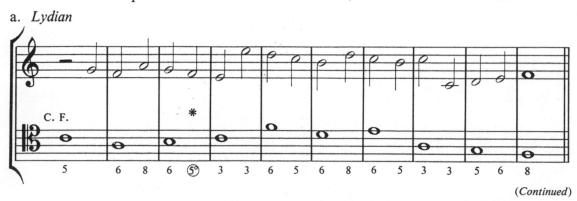

(*Continued*)

* The 5° indicates a diminished 5th. The student should distinguish carefully between the consonant perfect 5th and the dissonant diminished 5th.

b. *Mixolydian transposed*

c. *Aeolian*

d. *Dorian*

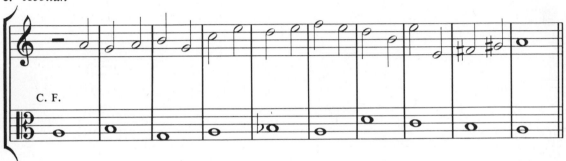

e. *Phrygian*

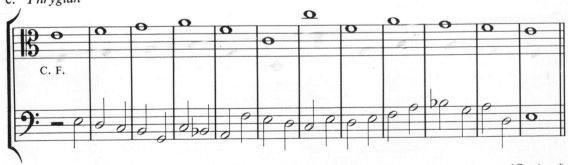

(Continued)

f. *Ionian transposed*

Assignment V

Write a counterpoint in Second Species above each of the following C. F.'s. Transpose at least one of them.

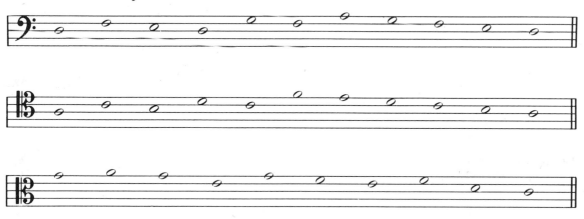

Assignment VI

Write a counterpoint in Second Species below each of the following C. F.'s. Transpose at least one of them.

Third Species in Two Parts

MELODIC PRINCIPLES

In quarter-note texture strong and weak quarters alternate, and the weak quarters are described as "off the beats". The first quarter is the primary accent, the third quarter is the secondary accent.

1. The Third Species voice should enter on the second quarter after a quarter rest.

2. All melodic principles previously stated should be followed, except that now two leaps in the same direction should be avoided.

3. An upward leap from a first or third quarter should be avoided, since such a leap displaces the melodic accent.

4. After a leap of a 4th or more, the melody should return in the opposite direction to the leap.

5. Each measure of four quarters should have at least one stepwise move. This does not apply to the opening and some penultimate measures. (See No. 7 under Harmonic Principles, p. 25.)

6. Previous recommendations concerning good use of range, climax points, and avoidance of repeated patterns should still be observed.

7. The melodic interval of an augmented 4th on successive beats should be avoided unless the melodic movement has changed direction. Altering one tone in the intervals, preferably the second, solves the problem.

Example 25

HARMONIC PRINCIPLES

1. In Third Species, or four quarter notes against each note in the C. F., the first and third quarters must be consonant.

2. Dissonant passing tones and lower auxiliaries may be used on second and fourth quarters. Dissonant upper auxiliaries should be avoided.

3. The unison may be used anywhere in Third Species except on a primary accent.

4. Parallel octaves and parallel 5ths must be avoided between the first, third, or fourth quarter of one measure and the first of the next. But 5ths in contrary motion are correct on successive beats.

Example 26

5. The Nota Cambiata, abbreviated N. C., is perhaps the most characteristic idiom of Renaissance music.

Melodically, it is a five-note figure consisting of a downward step, followed by a downward leap of a 3rd, followed by two upward steps. It may begin on either the first or third quarter of a measure.

Harmonically, the first, third, and fifth quarters must be consonant; the others may be dissonant, even the one left by downward leap. This is the only idiom where a leap away from a dissonance was practised in this style. Parallel octaves or fifths on successive primary accents are correct in this figure.

Example 27

6. Opening intervals should, as in previous species, be

   a. above the C. F., a perfect octave, 5th or unison
   b. below the C. F., a perfect octave or unison.

7. At the cadence the penultimate measure may contain, instead of four quarter notes, either a whole note, or two quarters and a half note. In any case, the next to the last note in the counterpoint will form a major 6th above the C. F. or a minor 3rd or minor 10th below it.

Example 28

Example 29. THIRD SPECIES IN TWO PARTS—MODEL EXAMPLES

a. *Lydian*

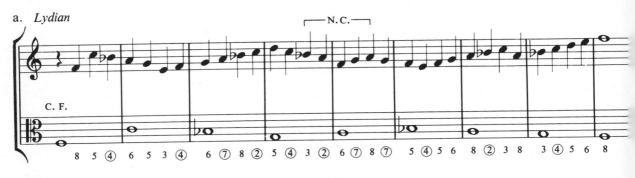

b. *Aeolian transposed*

c. *Ionian*

(Continued)

d. *Dorian*

e. *Phrygian transposed*

f. *Mixolydian*

Assignment VII

Write a counterpoint in Third Species above each of the following C. F.'s. Transpose at least one, and use at least one Nota Cambiata figure in the lesson.

Assignment VIII

Write a counterpoint in Third Species below each of the following C. F.'s. Transpose at least one, and use at least one Nota Cambiata figure in the lesson.

Fourth Species in Two Parts

MELODIC PRINCIPLES

1. Fourth Species, the study of syncopation, consists of two half notes against a whole note of the C. F., but the second of the two half notes should usually be tied into the next strong beat.

2. Because of the halting rhythm, melodic rules governing successive skips may be ignored.

3. The Fourth Species voice will begin after a half rest.

HARMONIC PRINCIPLES

1. The first of the two tied half notes must always be consonant.

2. The half note to which it is tied may be either consonant or dissonant. If consonant, it is called a tied concord.

3. If the second of the tied half notes is a dissonance, it should be treated as a suspension and should resolve downward by step to an imperfect consonance.

4. a. When the counterpoint is above the C. F., the suspensions available in two parts are the intervals 4–3 and 7–6.

   b. When the counterpoint is below, there is only one suspension available: 2–3, and its compound, 9–10, which should also be analyzed 2–3. In Example 30 *P* stands for preparation, *S* for suspension, and *R* for resolution.

Example 30

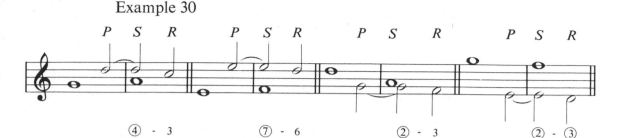

5. Unisons may be used on either beat in Fourth Species.

6. If continuous syncopation is impossible, Second Species may be used for one measure, but for no more than one measure at a time.

7. Since it is desirable to maintain syncopation, a chain of similar suspensions often occurs. Consequently the rule prohibiting the number of successive 3rds and 6ths is not applied here.

8. In uninterrupted syncopation octaves or 5ths on successive strong beats are correct; neither are they wrong on successive weak beats in two-part counterpoint. But if the syncopation is broken, octaves or 5ths on successive strong beats should be avoided, just as in Second Species.

Example 31

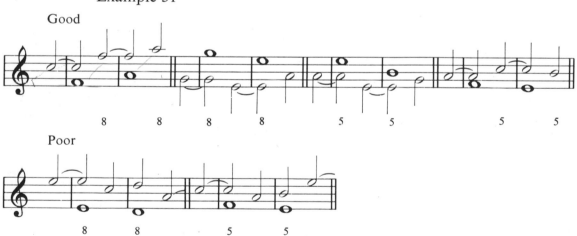

9. Direct octaves and 5ths will not occur in Fourth Species, since the voices do not move simultaneously.

10. In analysis of model examples and the student's own studies, it is recommended that figures for suspensions be circled.

11. Some of the possible cadences are shown in Example 32. Those with suspensions are preferred to those with syncopated concords.

Example 32

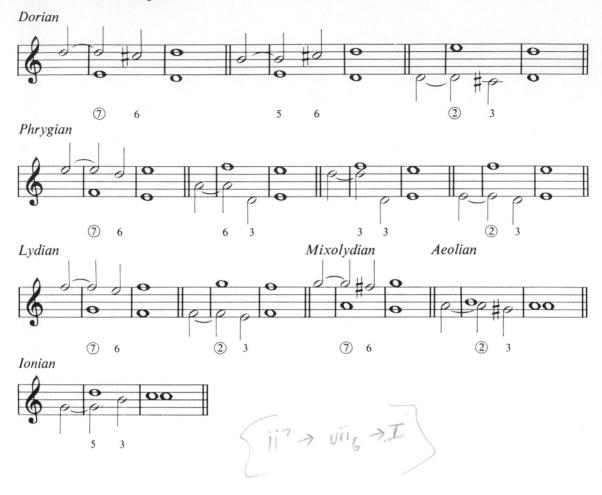

Dorian

Phrygian

Lydian   *Mixolydian*   *Aeolian*

Ionian

Example 33. FOURTH SPECIES IN TWO PARTS—MODEL EXAMPLES

a. *Lydian*

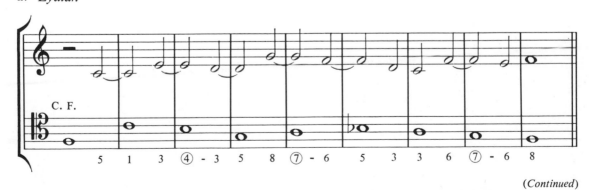

C. F.

5   1   3   ④ - 3   5   8   ⑦ - 6   5   3   3   6   ⑦ - 6   8

(Continued)

b. *Mixolydian transposed*

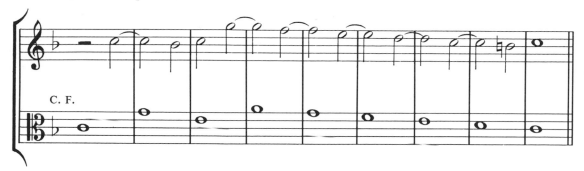

c. *Aeolian*

d. *Ionian*

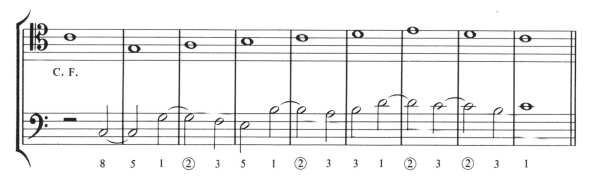

e. *Dorian*

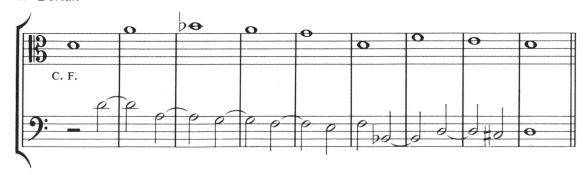

(*Continued*)

f. *Phrygian transposed*

C. F.

Assignment IX

Write a counterpoint in Fourth Species above each of the following C. F.'s.
Transpose at least one.

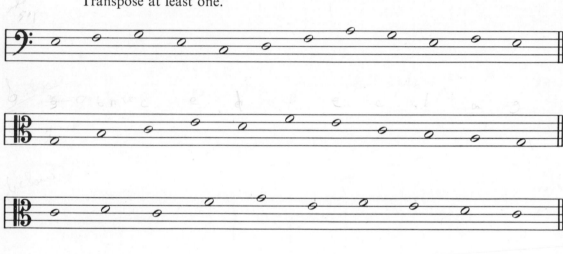

Assignment X

Write a counterpoint in Fourth Species below the following C. F.'s. Transpose at
least one.

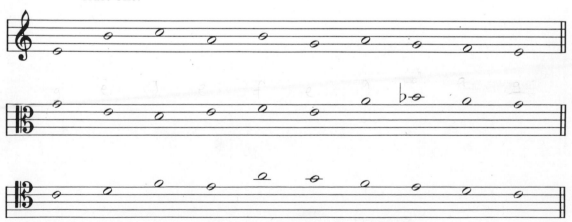

Fifth Species in Two Parts

MELODIC PRINCIPLES

1. Fifth Species is a combination of all the species previously studied, plus certain new resources, including eighth notes, dotted half notes, and ornamental resolutions of suspensions.

2. Eighth notes should be used as follows:

    a. in conjunct pairs, approached and left by step

    b. on second or fourth quarters only

    c. no more than one pair at a time

    d. no more than one pair in a measure

    e. not in successive measures.

3. Upper auxiliaries in eighth notes should be avoided, but lower auxiliaries are good on either the first or second eighth of a pair.

4. No more than ten quarter notes, or quarter notes and pairs of eighths, should be used in succession.

5. After two quarter notes, or one quarter and a pair of eighths, in the first half of the measure, a half note on the second half must be tied over.

6. The first of two tied notes must always be a half note.

7. This preparation note may be tied to a half note, or, when an ornamental resolution is used, to a quarter, as shown in Example 38. In all cases of tied notes, no matter whether the second is dissonant or consonant, the ratio of the first to the second must be either one-to-one or two-to-one. Thus a note must never be tied to one that is longer than itself.

8. Dotted half notes should not be left by upward leap. (step ok)

9. Several incorrect melodic patterns are illustrated in Example 34, numbered to correspond to the items under MELODIC PRINCIPLES.

Example 34

All Poor

10. Mixture of species within the measure is desirable, as well as variety of rhythms in successive measures.

11. It is desirable to open with either Second or Fourth Species.

12. Again, good use of range, climactic high and low points, and avoidance of repeated patterns make for a good style.

HARMONIC PRINCIPLES

1. After a half note on the strong beat, a dissonant quarter in descending progression is correct on the third quarter if it moves on downward in scale-steps to a consonance. The dissonant quarter is called a relatively accented downward passing tone.

Example 35

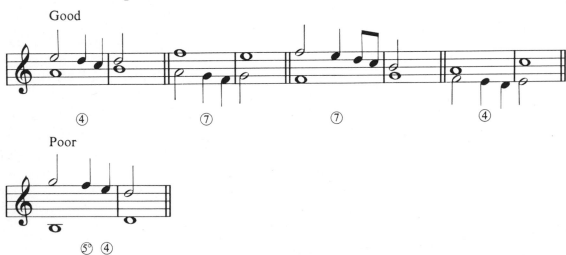

2. An upper auxiliary quarter note on the second quarter is correct when followed by a tied half note.

Example 36

3. The Nota Cambiata is now available in notes of mixed values, but in this case the first note may not be shorter than a dotted half, and the second must be a quarter note. If the third note is a quarter note, the full five-note pattern must be used (Example 37a), but if the third note is a half note, the pattern is considered complete with four notes (Example 37b).

Example 37

4. Anticipations or embellishments of the resolutions of suspensions are of four types, shown in Example 38. They all require that the suspension resolve on the third quarter (see Example 38e).

- a. anticipation
- b. eighth-note auxiliary
- c. downward leap of a 3rd to a consonant interval
- d. repetition of the dissonant tone.

Example 38

5. The anticipation may also be used to ornament any stepwise downward progression, and is not limited to resolutions of a suspension.

6. A variety of cadences is possible. They may be drawn from any species, but those using suspensions are preferred:

Example 39

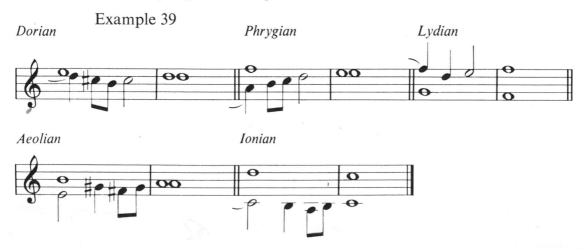

Example 40. FIFTH SPECIES IN TWO PARTS—MODEL EXAMPLES

a. *Dorian transposed*

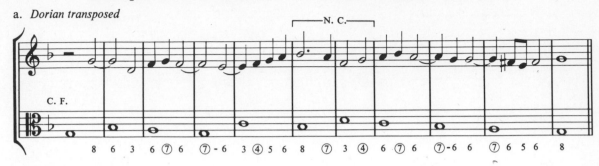

b. *Lydian transposed*

c. *Aeolian*

d. *Phrygian*

e. *Mixolydian transposed*

f. *Ionian*

Assignment XI

Write a counterpoint in Fifth Species above each of the following C. F.'s. Transpose at least one.

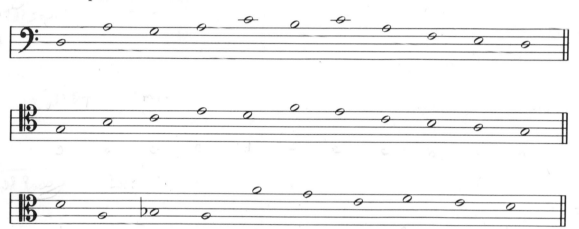

Assignment XII

Write a counterpoint in Fifth Species below each of the following C. F.'s. Transpose at least one.

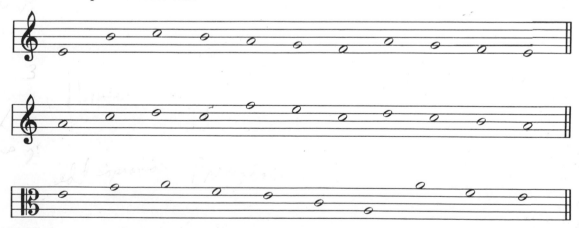

CHAPTER 3

Three-Part Counterpoint

[handwritten in margin: D not use ⁶₄ chord]

1. With the addition of a third voice it becomes possible to use complete triads. The harmonic vocabulary is limited, however, to consonant combinations, which will be analyzed in two ways: as intervals above the bass and as triad structures:

Intervals	Triads
a. Major 3rd and perfect 5th	Major triad in root position
b. Minor 3rd and perfect 5th	Minor triad in root position
c. Minor 3rd and minor 6th	Major triad in first inversion
d. Major 3rd and major 6th	Minor triad in first inversion
e. Minor 3rd and major 6th	Diminished triad in first inversion.

The student should note that the intervals of a perfect 4th, augmented 4th, and diminished 5th, which will occur between upper parts in combinations c, d, and e, are not reckoned as discords. But when these intervals occur between the *bass* and an upper part, they are discords.

2. The "white-key" notes and B♭ make the following triads available in untransposed modes:

Example 41

The use of F♯, C♯, or G♯, either as leading tone or Tierce de Picardie, makes the following triads available at cadences:

Example 42

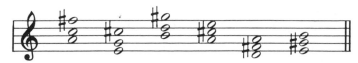

39

In addition to its melodic usefulness in avoiding a leap of an augmented 4th, F♯ may now be used to avoid a diminished triad in root position on B. F♯ is not so freely used as B♭ however, for F♯ almost always moves to G or G♯, whereas B♭ may move upward or downward, by leap or step.

Example 43

3. Here is a resumé of accidentals available in modal writing in three or more parts:

B♭ is used

a. between two A's.

b. often, but not always, descending to A.

c. in or near the Lydian and Dorian cadences.

d. in the signature of a transposed mode.

e. to avoid a melodic tritone F to B, or a diminished triad in root position, especially in the Dorian, Lydian and Mixolydian.

E♭ is used

in transposed modes only, just as B♭ is in untransposed modes.

F♯ is used

a. as leading tone in the Mixolydian and transposed Dorian.

b. as Tierce de Picardie in the Dorian and transposed Aeolian.

c. as raised 6th in the Aeolian mode.

d. occasionally to avoid a melodic tritone or a diminished triad on B.

C♯ is used

a. as leading tone in Dorian and transposed Aeolian.

b. as Tierce de Picardie in Aeolian and transposed Phrygian.

G♯ is used

a. as leading tone in the Aeolian.

b. as Tierce de Picardie in the Phrygian.

4. Chords may be used in either close or extended positions. Because of the desirability of free melodic movement, the distances between adjacent parts may occasionally be more than an octave, if not for too extended a passage and if each voice is singing in its own suitable and comfortable range. In general, however, equidistance of parts is best, and if a wider gap is necessary, it should occur between the two lower, rather than between the two upper parts.

5. METHOD OF PROCEDURE: Within the limits of the available chordal vocabulary, a note of the C. F. in the bass may be treated only as root or third of a triad; but in either upper part it may be treated as root, third or fifth of a triad, and that triad may be either in root position or in first inversion. Thus there are six possibilities for a note of the C. F. in either middle or top part.

*Dim. chord
use in 1st inv.*

Incomplete triads are available, though they are not as desirable as complete triads, and all tones may be doubled freely except at a cadence, where the leading tone may not be doubled. Doubling of a leading tone elsewhere is not objectionable. (Remember that F is the leading tone of the Phrygian mode and should not be doubled at a cadence.)

In Example 44 the whole note represents the C. F.; the stemless black notes are the available tones in the counterpoint.

Example 44

C in the bass

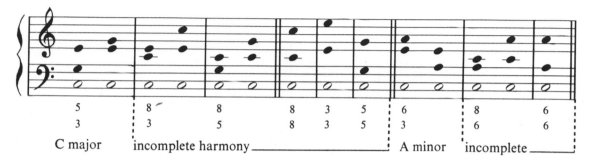

C in an upper voice

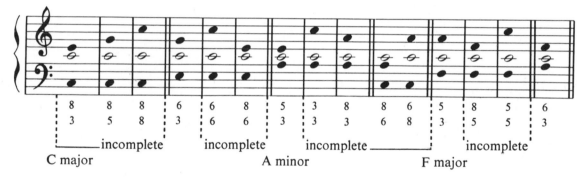

6. Analysis of all model examples and of the student's studies is vital. In such analysis, the lowest tone sounded determines the position of the chord, no matter what voice sounds it.

7. The following METHOD OF ANALYSIS is recommended as an aid for testing both voice-leading and harmonic correctness:

 a. Below the bass line, write the figures that represent the *intervals above the bass*, the upper row showing intervals between soprano and bass, the lower row those between middle part and bass. Incorrect consecutives between bass and upper parts will become apparent, as in Example 45a.

b. Above the bass line, indicate the triads in the following way, which shows the root and the structure:

A capital letter indicates a major triad.

A small letter indicates a minor triad.

A small letter with a small circle to the right of it indicates a diminished triad.

The number 6 indicates a first inversion.

Example 45

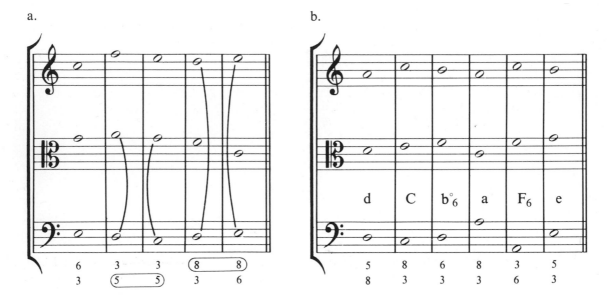

CAUTIONS:

1. The figures below the bass will not reveal the faulty consecutives between upper parts. These voices must be tested separately.

Example 46

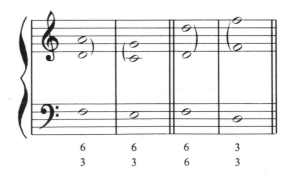

2. The student should be especially careful to avoid the familiar but faulty constructions shown in Example 47.

Example 47

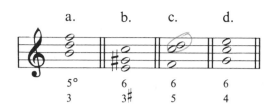

a. The diminished 5th above the bass is a dissonance.

b. No dissonant intervals above the bass appear, but the augmented triad is dissonant.

c. Again no dissonant intervals appear in the figures, but the total effect is dissonant.

d. The 4th above the bass is dissonant.

Augmented triads in first inversion were occasionally used by Renaissance composers to express such words as grief, tears, death, anguish, etc., but the student should not use them in studies without text.

First Species in Three Parts

1. Consecutive octaves and 5ths in parallel motion must, of course, be avoided. Octaves as well as 5ths in contrary motion, however, are now permissible.

2. The progression of a diminished 5th to a perfect 5th in upper parts is correct when the second triad is in first inversion.

Example 48

3. Direct 5ths and octaves are freely allowed between an outer and an inner voice, but between outer voices only if the upper voice moves by step, or when there is no change of chord. Direct unisons should be avoided.

Example 49

Good   Poor

4. Unisons of any two voices may be written anywhere, but all three voices in unison may occur only in the first measure.

5. If the student wishes to imitate the first few notes of the C. F., entries of the counterpoints may be deferred, but the first harmonic interval heard should be a perfect consonance, as in two parts.

6. Unless there is imitation, the three voices will enter simultaneously, in which case the possible openings are:

    a. three roots
    b. root, root and fifth; or root, fifth and fifth
    c. root, third and fifth.

 NOTE that if the third is present, the fifth must be also, and this complete triad must be major. It is usable only if its root is the Final of the mode.

7. Doubling of the leading tone in the cadence is not good. In the Phrygian mode this note is F. It may be said that there is no function of leading tone until the penultimate measure.

8. The cadence in three-part counterpoint has the same intervals as a two-part cadence plus an added voice. This added note in the last chord, if it is the 3rd of the chord, must be a major 3rd; and if it is not so naturally, it must be sharped (TIERCE DE PICARDIE), specifically, in the Dorian, Phrygian, and Aeolian modes. The cadences in Example 50 illustrate what the added notes in the semi-final chords should be.

Example 50

Example 51. FIRST SPECIES IN THREE PARTS—MODEL EXAMPLES

a. *Mixolydian transposed*

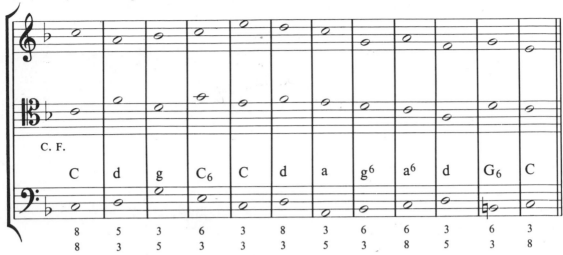

C. F.

C   d   g   C_6   C   d   a   g^6   a^6   d   G_6   C

8   5   3   6   3   8   3   6   6   3   6   3
8   3   5   3   3   3   5   3   8   5   3   8

b. *Mixolydian* (*imitative entries*)

C. F.

c. *Aeolian*

C. F. a   b°_6   C   G_6   a^6   b°_6   d_6   C_6   a   a^6   g♯°_6   A

5   3   3   6   6   3   6   8   3   6   6   8
8   6   8   3   3   6   3   3   8   3   3   3

(Continued)

d. *Lydian*

Assignment XIII

Use the following C. F. in three examples of First Species counterpoint in three parts, placing the C. F. once in the bottom voice, once in the middle, and once at the top, transposing it to other clefs as needed, and at least once to a one-flat signature, a 4th up or a 5th down.

Second Species in Three Parts

1. In the remaining species of three-part counterpoint, one of the free voices will be in First Species, the other in the characteristic species—in this lesson, untied half notes.

2. The first interval heard against the C. F. in the First Species voice should be perfect, and is governed by two-part rules.

3. The Second Species should enter after a half rest, on <u>either</u> a perfect or imperfect concord. *U.B.36.*

4. Rules relating to consecutive 5ths and octaves in two-part work should still be observed, except that perfect 5ths may now be used on successive strong beats when a different chord intervenes.

Example 52

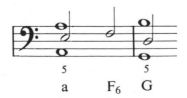

5   5

a F_6 G

5. Direct 5ths and octaves in outside voices may be used under circumstances described in First Species, provided the movement is made from concordant tones.

Example 53

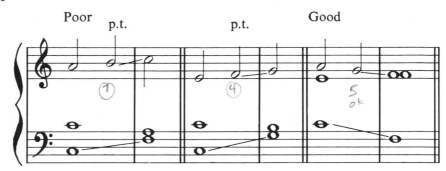

6. In the cadence, the leading tone may be used in either the First or the Second Species voice. It is permissible and often desirable to use a Fourth Species cadence at the close of a Second Species exercise, in which case the suspension is usually of the leading tone. Some of these are included in Example 54.

Example 54

Dorian

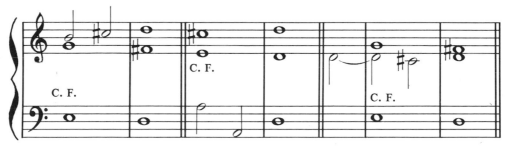

Phrygian

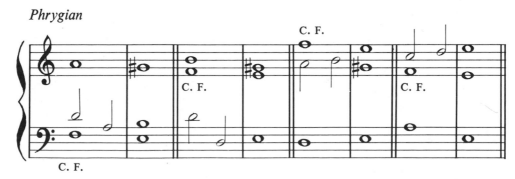

(Continued)

Lydian

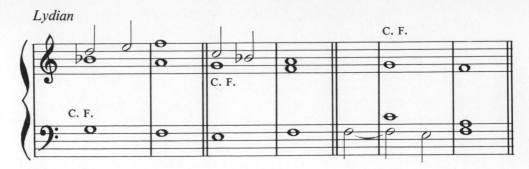

Mixolydian

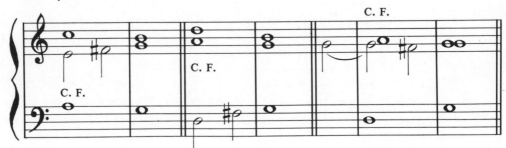

Aeolian

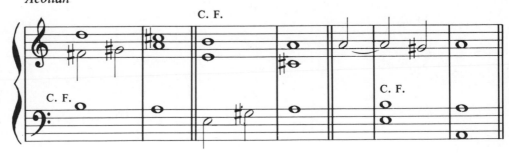

Ionian

Example 55. SECOND SPECIES IN THREE PARTS—MODEL EXAMPLES

a. *Phrygian transposed*

b. *Lydian transposed*

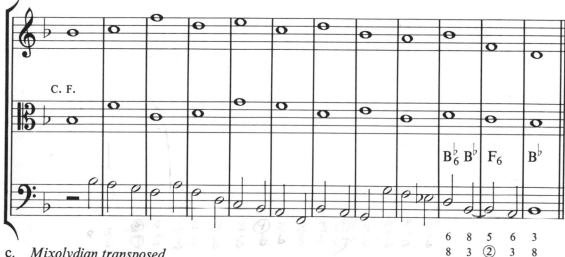

c. *Mixolydian transposed*

(Continued)

d. *Mixolydian*

Assignment XIV

To the following C. F. write three examples of Second Species counterpoint in three parts, using the C. F. once in each part and the Second Species once in each part, according to this plan:

2	1	C. F.
1	C. F.	2
C. F.	2	1

Third Species in Three Parts

1. After a perfect consonance has been heard between the C. F. and the First Species voice, the Third Species voice will begin after a quarter rest, on either a perfect or imperfect concord.

2. All the principles of Third Species counterpoint should be carefully reviewed.

3. Care must be taken to avoid faulty consecutives, both between the Third Species and the whole-note added voice, and between the Third Species and the C. F.

4. Progression from a 7th or 9th in similar motion to an octave should be avoided between the Third Species voice and either of the voices in whole notes (direct octave).

Example 56

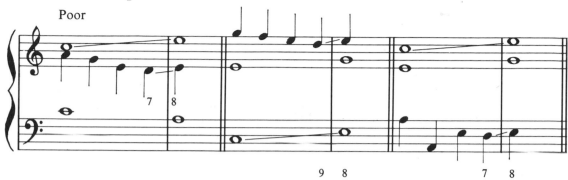

5. Some cadences are shown in Example 57. Where none of these will serve, a First or Second Species cadence may be used. Note the continued use of Tierce de Picardie.

Example 57

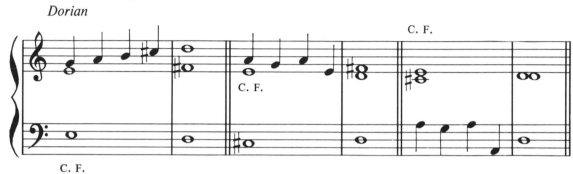

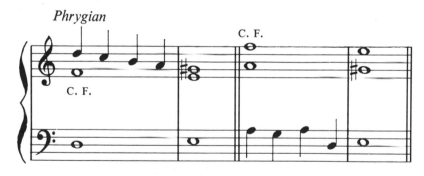

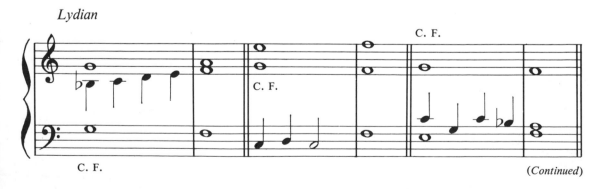

(Continued)

Mixolydian

Aeolian

Ionian

Example 58. THIRD SPECIES IN THREE PARTS—MODEL EXAMPLES

a. *Ionian transposed*

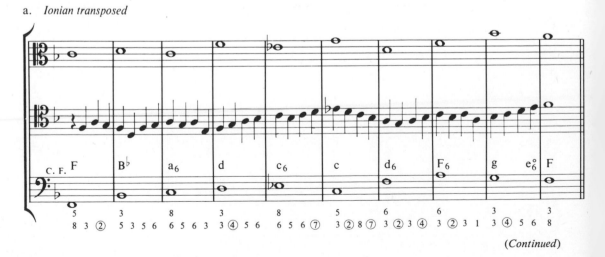

(Continued)

b. *Phrygian*

c. *Aeolian transposed*

d. *Phrygian transposed*

Assignment XV

To the following C. F. write three examples of three-part counterpoint, using the C. F. once in each part, and Third Species once in each part, according to the plan:

3	1	C. F.
1	C. F.	3
C. F.	3	1

Transpose the C. F. to other clefs as needed, and at least once a 4th up or a 5th down.

Fourth Species in Three Parts

1. After a perfect consonance has been heard between the C. F. and the other whole-note voice, the Fourth Species will begin after a half rest on any suitable concord.

2. Certain new resources are now available, in that suspensions not correct in two-part counterpoint are usable in three parts provided they form an approved suspension with the other whole-note voice. The 9–8 suspension in one of the upper voices, and the 4–5 and 7–8 suspensions in the lowest voice thus become available as shown in Example 59.

Example 59

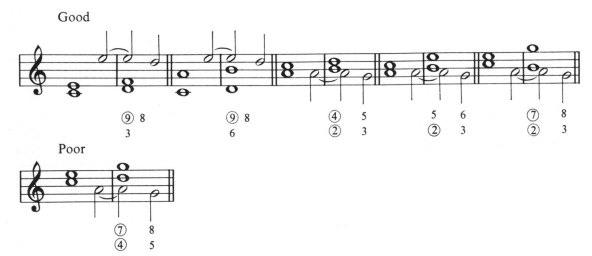

3. In general, a suspension should not be accompanied by the note of resolution—4–3 by a 3rd, and 7–6 by a 6th. Exceptions to this occur when the 7th is at least a major 9th above the 6th, and resolution is to a major or minor triad in first inversion.

4. Specifically, when the Fourth Species is in an upper part:

    a. the 4–3 suspension should be accompanied by a 5th, 6th, or octave.

    b. the 7–6 suspension should be accompanied by a 3rd, an octave, or conditionally by a 6th.

    c. the 9–8 suspension should be accompanied by a 3rd or a 6th.

Example 60

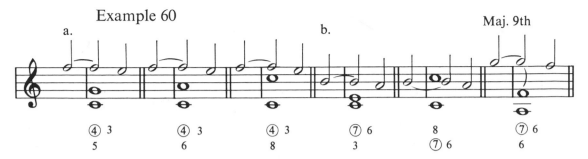

Example 60 (continued)

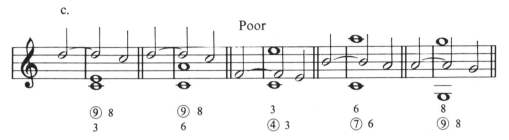

5. When the Fourth Species forms the lowest part:

    a. the 2–3 suspension should be accompanied by a 2nd, 4th, 5th, or 7th.

    b. the 7–8 suspension should be accompanied by a 2nd or 5th.

Example 61

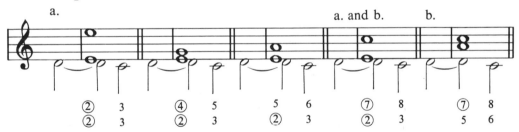

6. Now that the 9–8 suspension has become available, it is necessary to make a clear distinction between the two uses of the interval of a 9th: these are (a) when the upper note is the suspension, and (b) when the lower note is the suspension.

    a. A suspension in an upper voice is always indicated by the figure 9, and this may never be reduced to a second.

    b. A suspension in the bass is always indicated by the figure 2, though the interval may often be an actual 9th.

Example 62

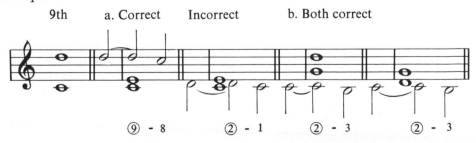

7. A WARNING: The 9–8 suspension is not good at the cadence over the leading tone.

8. Where suspension is impractical, syncopation should be maintained as long as possible by tying over to concordant tones.

9. To sum up, all suspensions must resolve downward scalewise into one of the five concordant combinations—complete or incomplete, but containing a 3rd or a 6th—and all half notes except the suspensions themselves will be consonant.

10. Consecutives resulting from syncopation

    a. on successive strong beats are correct

    b. but care must be exercised on successive weak beats, where undesirable consecutives might result from resolution of a dissonance to an octave or perfect 5th. Octaves or perfect 5ths on weak beats of successive measures are incorrect when the intervening chord is dissonant, but correct when it is consonant. When the second 5th is diminished the consecutives are of course correct.

Example 63

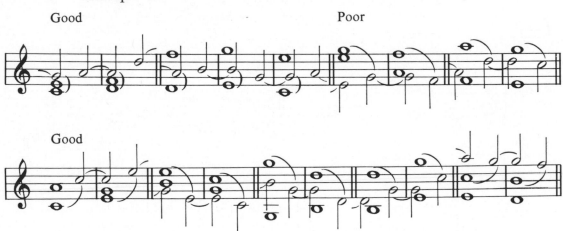

11. In an idiom characteristic of the 16th century, a 4–3 suspension over a repeated or tied note in the bass may be prepared by a 4th. This is the single instance in which a perfect 4th between the bass and an upper part is used as a consonant interval, and it always occurs over a stationary bass. The idiom is called a consonant 4th.

Example 64

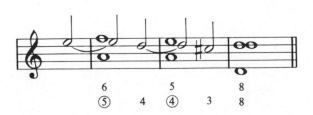

12. Cadences are again shown in each of the modes.

Example 65

Dorian

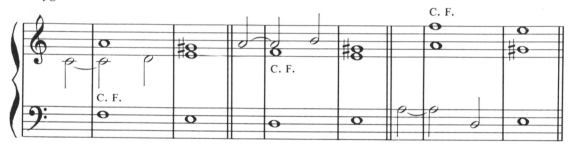

Phrygian

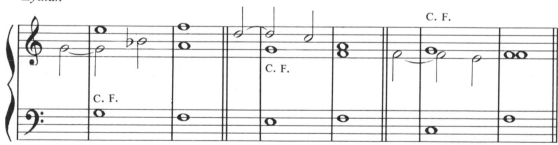

Lydian

Mixolydian

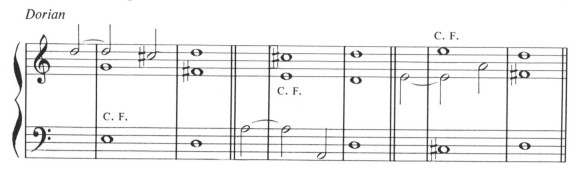

(Continued)

Aeolian

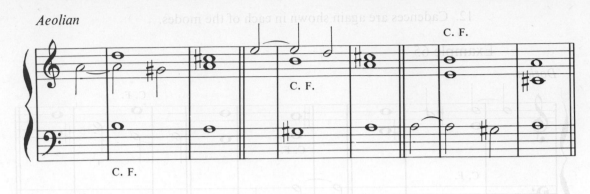

Ionian

Example 66. FOURTH SPECIES IN THREE PARTS—MODEL EXAMPLES

a. *Ionian transposed*

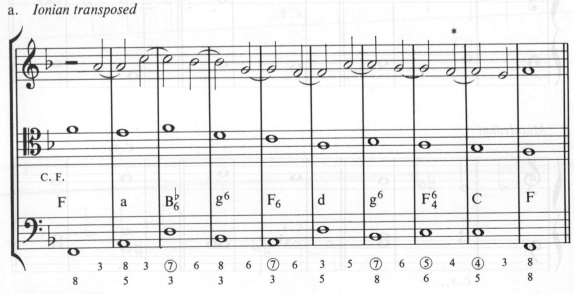

*Consonant 4th

(Continued)

b. *Mixolydian*

c. *Lydian*

d. *Phrygian*

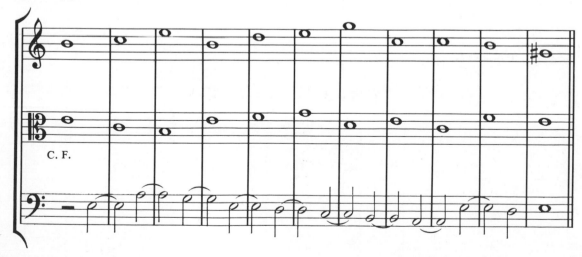

Assignment XVI

To the following C. F. write three examples of three-part counterpoint, placing the C. F. once in each part and Fourth Species once in each part. At least one transposed form of the C. F. should be used, as well as change of clef when needed:

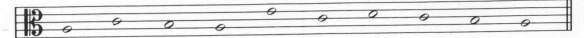

Fifth Species in Three Parts

1. Although no new principles need to be stated, the student must not neglect to re-study the chapter on Fifth Species in two parts to refresh his mind on the proper use of eighth notes, resolution of suspensions, etc. Remember that a melody in Fifth Species begins with a half note, tied or untied.

2. Cadences given in the chapter on Fifth Species in two parts, if compared with subsequently given three-part cadences, will suggest a wealth of good procedures. Study and analysis of the model examples are also of prime importance.

Example 67. FIFTH SPECIES IN THREE PARTS—MODEL EXAMPLES

a. *Dorian transposed*

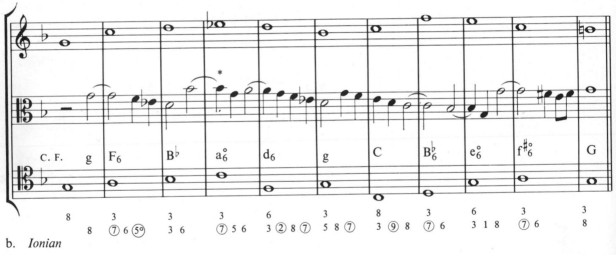

b. *Ionian*

* The student should name the idioms marked with asterisks.

(*Continued*)

c. *Mixolydian transposed*

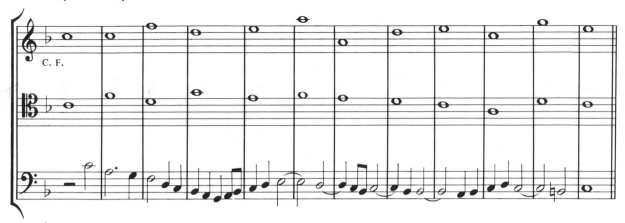

d. *Phrygian transposed*

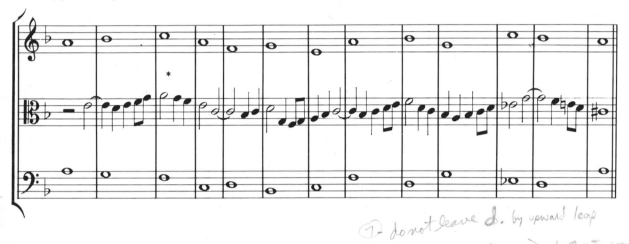

7. do not leave d. by upward leap

use N.C. (5 note figure) 1-3-5 cons.

Assignment XVII

To the following C. F. write three examples of three-part counterpoint, placing
the C. F. once in each voice and Fifth Species once in each voice. Use the C. F. at
least once in transposed form.

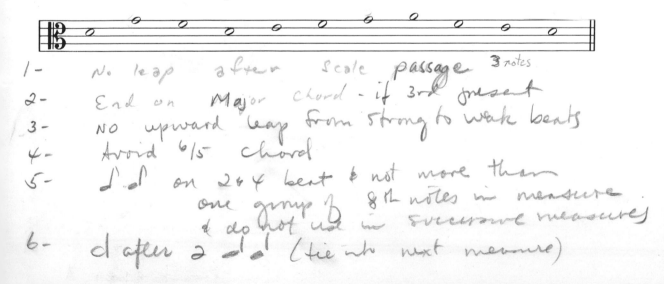

1- No leap after scale passage 3 notes

2- End on Major chord - if 3rd present

3- NO upward leap from strong to weak beats

4- Avoid 6/5 chord

5- ♩.♩ on 2 & 4 beat & not more than
     one group of 8th notes in measure
     & do not use in successive measures

6- d after 2 ♩.♩ (tie into next measure)

CHAPTER 4

Combined Counterpoint in Three Parts

When two parts in any two different species except First are combined with a C. F. some new resources become available, and the texture gains in contrapuntal interest.

Second and Third Species Combined

1. The Third Species voice should begin on the second quarter of the first measure after a quarter rest, and the Second Species voice on the second half after a half rest.

2. The first voice heard against the C. F.—in this case, the Third Species—must always form with it a perfect consonant interval. This will hold true in all future combined counterpoint. The remaining voice may then enter on any suitable consonance, perfect or imperfect.

3. The three voices must form consonant triads on every beat, whether strong or weak. No passing tone in half notes is therefore available.   *1 - 3*

4. Consecutives:

    a. Consecutives on successive first beats between the C. F. and either moving voice are correct when a different triad intervenes, but not otherwise

    b. between the Second and Third Species voices consecutives are incorrect on successive beats   *1-3 or 3-1*

    c. between the Second and Third Species voices consecutives are correct on (1) first beats of successive measures, or (2) when a member of the second 5th is a passing tone.

63

Example 68

5. In cadences, borrowings from Fourth Species are again correct in the Second Species voice.

Example 69

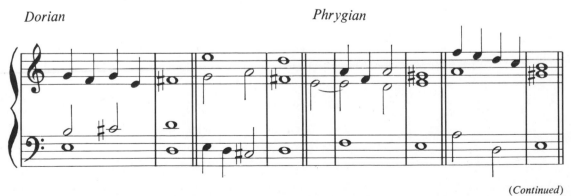

(Continued)

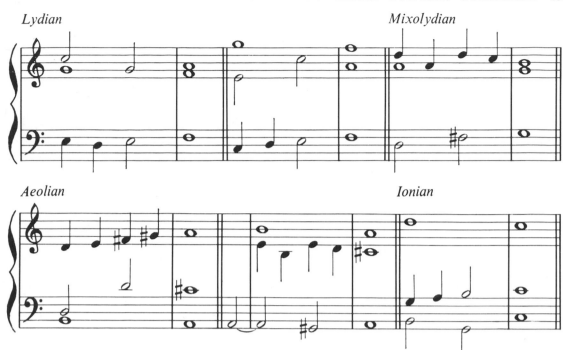

Example 70. SECOND AND THIRD SPECIES COMBINED—MODEL EXAMPLES

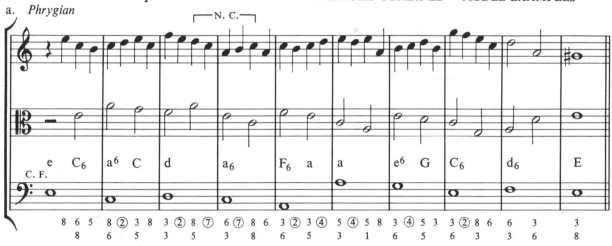

(Continued)

c. *Mixolydian*

d. *Dorian*

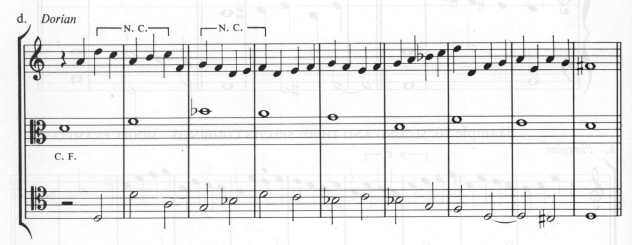

Assignment XVIII

To the following C. F. write three examples of Second and Third Species combined counterpoint according to the plan:

3	2	C. F.
2	C. F.	3
C. F.	3	2

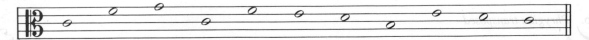

Second and Fourth Species Combined

1. In order to avoid simultaneous entries of the Second and Fourth Species, the beginning of either one may be delayed until the second half of the second measure. In combined species it is better to defer an entry one or two measures than to have parts enter together.

2. New Resources: The motion of the Second Species may now

   a. shift the resolution of a suspension from root position to first inversion of a triad, or vice versa

   b. cause resolution on a new harmony

   c. produce good harmony where a consonant combination would have been impossible without motion on the second beat. This makes available the new prepared discords shown in Example 71—to be analyzed as seventh chords with prepared seventh:

      (1) a prepared 5th accompanied by a 6th. The 5th may be perfect or diminished; in either case it is dissonant with the 6th and must be prepared

      (2) a prepared 7th accompanied by a perfect 5th

      (3) a 4/2 chord which would have resolved on a diminished triad if the 4th above the bass had been a whole note.

   d. Note that a prepared seventh may be analyzed in one of two ways: as a suspension, or as the seventh of a seventh chord. The following test reveals which analysis is appropriate:

      (1) When the note of resolution, put in place of the prepared discord, results in a first inversion of a triad, the prepared discord is a suspension

      (2) When this momentary substitution results in another seventh chord, or in any other form of dissonant harmony, the prepared discord is the seventh of a seventh chord, as shown in Example 71.

Example 71

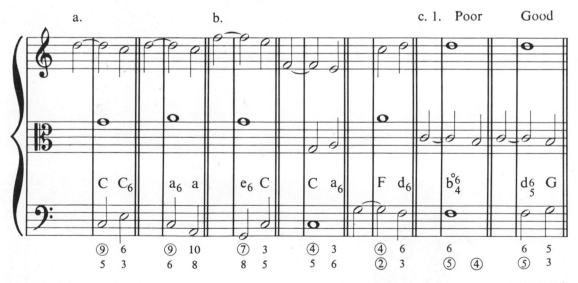

(Continued)

> *a suspens not accompanied by its resolution*

Notice that in each case the two notes struck together at the beginning of the measure are consonant with each other, and at the moment of resolution all parts unite to form a consonant triad.

3. A 9–8 suspension may now be prepared by an octave if the bass moves at the moment of resolution. However, the 9–8 suspension above the leading tone is still to be avoided at the cadence.

Example 72

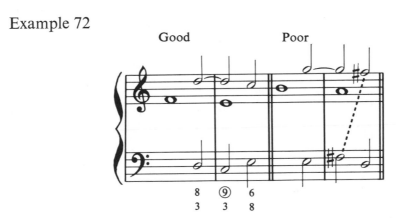

4. To identify correct and incorrect illustrations in Example 73, recall Rule 3, page 54.

Example 73

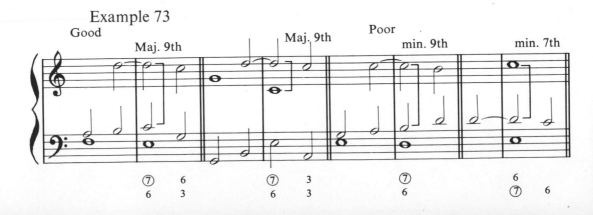

5. No two parts may approach an octave or a unison in similar motion if one of them is resolving a suspension.

Example 74

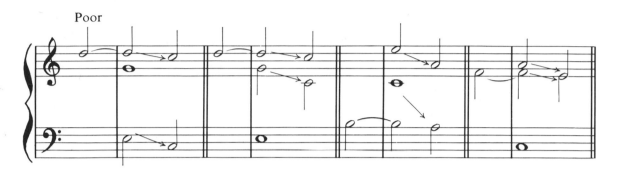

6. When a correct approach to the cadence proves impossible, Second Species may be used in both parts at once, or First Species in one of the added parts. A cadence is shown in each mode.

Example 75

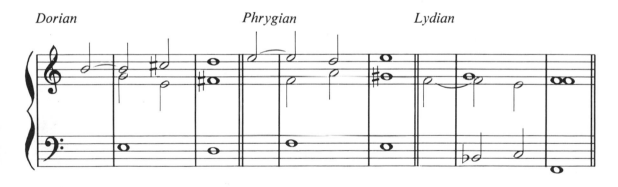

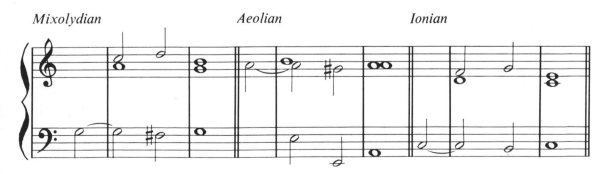

Example 76. SECOND AND FOURTH SPECIES COMBINED—MODEL EXAMPLES

a. *Lydian transposed*

b. *Aeolian*

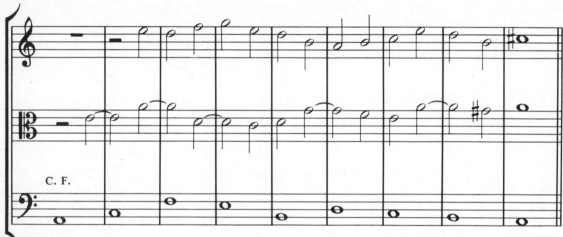

c. *Dorian transposed*

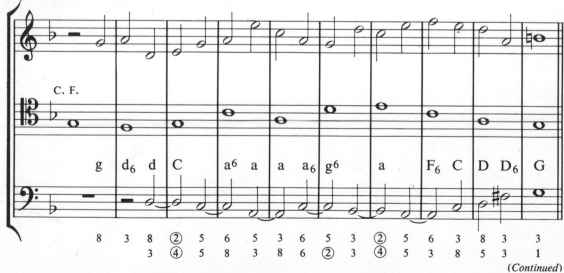

(Continued)

d. *Aeolian*

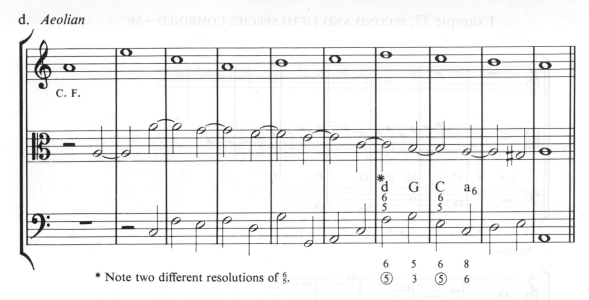

* Note two different resolutions of $^6_5$.

Assignment XIX

Write three examples of Second and Fourth Species combined, using the following C. F. and plan:

4	2	C. F.
2	C. F.	4
C. F.	4	2

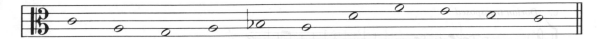

Second and Fifth Species Combined

1. Obviously, a number of successive untied half notes in the Fifth Species voice will be sadly lacking in rhythmic contrast in this combination. Rather than going to the opposite extreme of too much activity, the student is advised more strongly than ever to mix the species *within* the bar.

2. When the Second Species is in the bass, a good deal of disjunct movement is inevitable, and frequent changes of harmony will result.

3. From this point on, passing tones, auxiliaries, and ornamental resolutions need not be indicated in the analysis figures, though the student must always be able to identify them and take them into account in checking his work. Suspensions and relatively accented passing tones should still be shown in the figures, however. Note that a perfect 5th or a 6th occurring on the second or fourth quarter may be analyzed as a passing tone when it is approached and left by step.

4. Cadences are left to the student's own devising, but it is recommended that syncopation be used in the Fifth Species voice where possible.

Example 77. SECOND AND FIFTH SPECIES COMBINED—MODEL EXAMPLES

Assignment XX

To the following C. F. write three examples of Second and Fifth Species combined according to the following plan:

```
        5        2       C. F.
        2       C. F.      5
      C. F.      5         2
```

Third and Fourth Species Combined

1. Extension of the new resources of combined counterpoint, previously mentioned in Rule 2, page 67, adds the prepared discords illustrated in Example 78:

Example 78

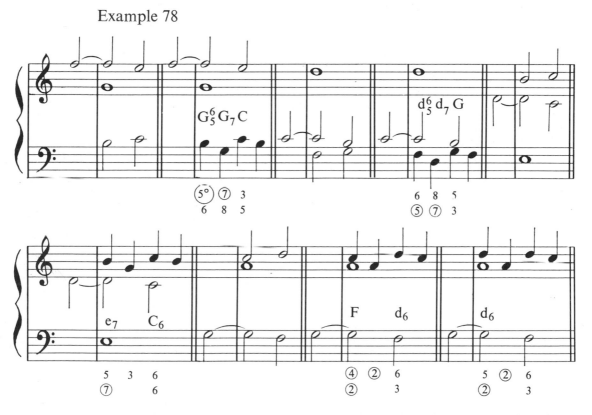

2. In general, a tone of resolution should not be heard in the Third Species voice against a suspension, except the special case for the 7–6, (Rule 3, page 54) and, of course, the 9–8 and 7–8.

Example 79

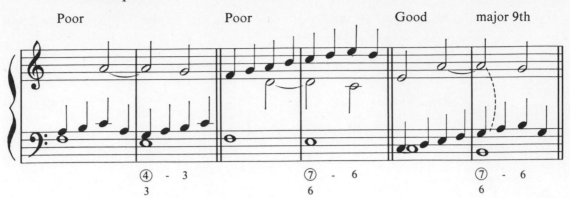

3. Two of the cadences given in Example 69 are usable here. Another for each mode is provided in Example 80.

Example 80

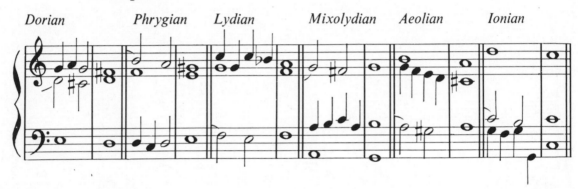

Example 81. THIRD AND FOURTH SPECIES COMBINED—MODEL EXAMPLES

a. *Phrygian transposed*

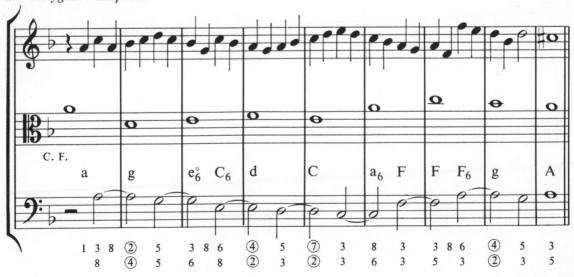

(Continued)

b. *Dorian*

c. *Aeolian transposed*

d. *Dorian*

Assignment XXI

Write three examples of Third and Fourth Species combined, using the following C. F. and plan:

3	4	C. F.
4	C. F.	3
C. F.	3	4

Third and Fifth Species Combined

1. In this combination the Fifth Species should be somewhat less active than in other combinations—half notes more numerous, quarter notes fewer—because of the constant activity of the Third Species voice. An occasional whole note or whole note tied to a half may be used. But a whole note may not be tied to a quarter note, nor to a dotted half.

2. Where simultaneous motion in quarter notes occurs:

    a. the parts may move in parallel 3rds or 6ths, but not more than three should be used in succession

    b. the same passing tone or auxiliary may be struck by two voices off the beats in contrary motion

    c. two auxiliaries may form a discord on the second quarter of the measure

    d. off the beats, a passing tone may be either consonant or dissonant with a chordal tone against which it is struck.

Example 82

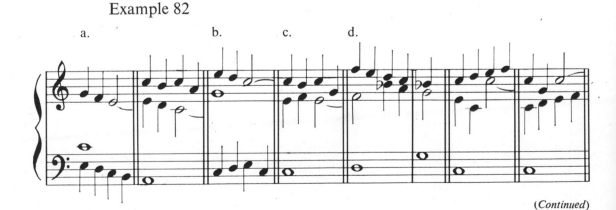

(*Continued*)

3. When eighth notes are used against a quarter note, either eighth may be dissonant.

Example 83

Good: First eighth consonant

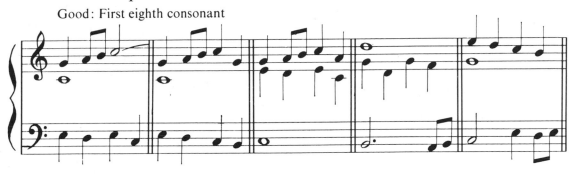

First eighth dissonant

4. Two of the cadences in Example 69 are usable here. Other cadences are given in Example 84.

Example 84

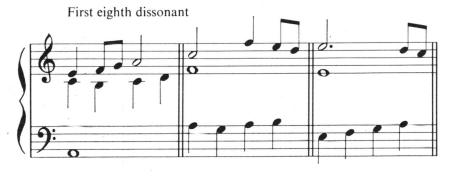

Dorian   *Phrygian*   *Lydian*   *Mixolydian*

(*Continued*)

Ionian   *Aeolian*

Example 85. THIRD AND FIFTH SPECIES COMBINED—MODEL EXAMPLES

a. *Phrygian*

b. *Phrygian*

c. *Dorian*

(Continued)

d. *Lydian*

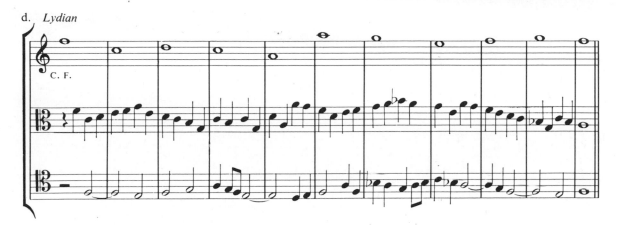

Assignment XXII

Write three examples of Third and Fifth Species combined using the following C. F. and transposing it at least once:

3	5	C. F.
5	C. F.	3
C. F.	3	5

Fourth and Fifth Species Combined

1. The Fifth Species part need not be consonant with the C. F. on the third quarter of the measure, provided it is consonant with the Fourth Species voice at the moment and forms a relatively accented downward passing tone after a half note.

Example 86

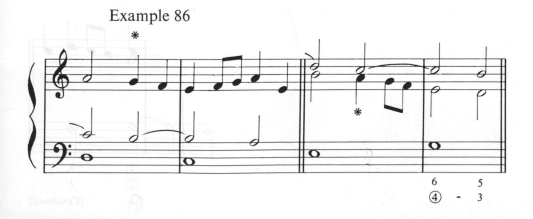

2. Double suspensions may be used, though they are infrequent in the style. Several are shown in Example 87.

Example 87

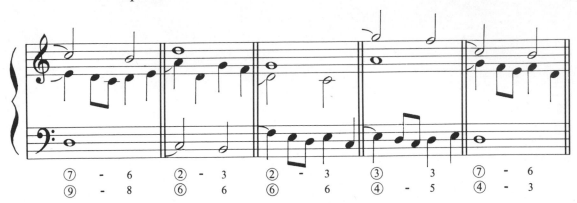

3. Further ornamentation of previously shown prepared discords (Rule 1, page 73) gives such possibilities as those in Example 88:

Example 88

(*Continued*)

$$\begin{array}{ccc} \textcircled{4} & 8 & 6 \\ \textcircled{2} & 3 & \end{array}$$

Example 89. FOURTH AND FIFTH SPECIES COMBINED—MODEL EXAMPLES

a. *Lydian transposed*

b. *Mixolydian*

c. *Phrygian transposed*

(Continued)

d. *Lydian*

Assignment XXIII

Write three examples of Fourth and Fifth Species combined using the following C. F. and transposing it at least once:

4	5	C. F.
5	C. F.	4
C. F.	4	5

Two Voices in Fifth Species

1. The technique in these final studies in three voices is a culmination of the work so far, and approaches an artistic realization of the style more nearly than the previous studies. The aims should be:

a. to obtain equally interesting melody in both voices in Fifth Species, which are called florid parts

b. to distribute activity as nearly as possible equally between them, avoiding too much simultaneous activity or inactivity.

2. The florid voices <u>should</u> now <u>enter with imitation</u>:

a. the imitation may be exact or free, that is, the size of a leap may be altered by a step or half step

b. the imitation may be similar or inverted

c. the imitation may be a rhythmic adaptation of the C. F. in smaller note values—a device called diminution.

Example 90

3. Eighth notes should rarely appear in two voices at once; if they do, they should move in parallel 3rds or 6ths.

Example 91

4. Simultaneous motion in half notes or quarter notes for more than a half measure is not best. Again, mixing the species within the measure is an excellent expedient.

Example 92. TWO VOICES IN FIFTH SPECIES—MODEL EXAMPLES

a. *Aeolian transposed*

C. F.

d a_6 F a_6 C_6 C G_6 e_6 e g B^b E_b d_6 d e_5^6 A D

1 6 3 6 6 8 3 6 3 8 5 ⑦ ⑨ 6 5 6 8 ⑤ 3 8
5 3 3 3 6 6 8 5 3 3 5 3 ⑦ 8 3 6 5 5

b. *Dorian*

C. F.

c. *Lydian*

C. F.

(Continued)

d. *Phrygian transposed*

Assignment XXIV

To the following C. F., placed once in the lowest, once in the middle, and once in the highest voice, add in each setting two florid parts illustrating imitative entries.

CHAPTER 5

Counterpoint in Triple Time

In the 16th century, "few compositions use triple time throughout", according to Gustave Soderlund in his *Direct Approach to Counterpoint in 16th Century Style* (New York, N. Y.: Appleton–Century–Crofts, Inc., 1947). "The main bulk is written in 4/2 time with incursions in either 3/1 or 3/2 time" (page 8). However, there are several points that should be understood before free writing is attempted.

Jeppesen tells us in his *Counterpoint* (page 119) that "triple time with the half note as the unit of measure requires, in the Palestrina style, that each half note be a consonance. . . . The rule is that in triple time only the second half of each unit of measure may be dissonant." Therefore in 3/2 time, only the quarters which fall off the beats may form dissonant intervals with the C. F. Since writing in half notes offers no new challenge, our exercises in triple time will begin with

Six Notes Against One
(Variant of Third Species)

1. The counterpoint will begin with a perfect concord after a quarter rest.

2. Passing tones and lower auxiliaries may be used off the beats.

3. The Nota Cambiata will be found useful with the downward leap of a 3rd occurring between fourth and fifth, or between sixth and first quarters of the measure. The first, third, and fifth notes of the Cambiata figure must be consonant. The Nota Cambiata outline may be used earlier in the measure, with downward leap from second to third quarter, though no leap from a dissonance occurs in this case.

Example 93

4. Some variety in the cadences is possible:

Example 94

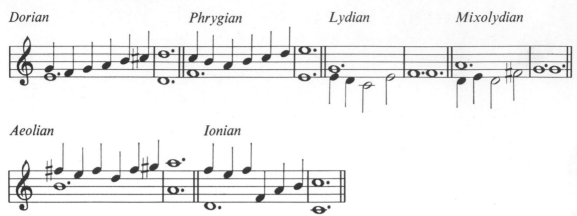

Syncopation
(Variant of Fourth Species)

1. The counterpoint will enter with a perfect concord after a half rest.

2. Syncopation occurs when the third half note of a measure is tied to the first half note of the next.

3. Suspensions will usually resolve upon the second half note of the measure. Resolution may, however, be deferred until the third half note if the ornamental resolution of 7–(5) 6, allowed in Fifth Species, is used. All half notes except the suspensions themselves must be consonant

Example 95

4. Some of the possible cadences are:

Example 96

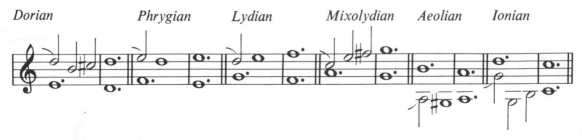

Florid Style
(Variant of Fifth Species)

1. Beginnings should be similar to those in Fifth Species in duple time, starting with a half note or tied half note after one or two half rests.

2. It is more than ever necessary to avoid excessive use of quarter and eighth notes, and to vary the species within the measure. A succession of measures of unmixed species, or two consecutive complete measures of any one species, is undesirable.

3. Resolution of suspensions on the third beat is made possible by embellishment of the resolution:

Example 97

4. Cadences should be formed with syncopation whenever possible.

Example 98. EXERCISES IN TRIPLE TIME—MODEL EXAMPLES
(six notes against one)

a. *Aeolian*

b. *Lydian*

Example 99. SYNCOPATION

a. *Ionian transposed*

(*Continued*)

b. *Lydian*

Example 100. FLORID STYLE

a. *Phrygian*

b. *Mixolydian*

Assignment XXV

Write one example of six notes against one above the first C. F., one example of syncopation in triple time below the second C. F., and two examples of florid style in triple time, one above and one below the given C. F.'s. Any previously given C. F. may be adapted to triple time by placing a dot after each note.

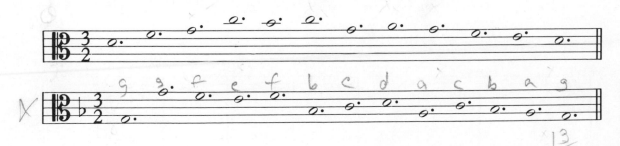

CHAPTER 6

Writing Without Cantus Firmus

In Two Parts

Although composing music on a given melody has been and will probably continue to be a part of a composer's practice as long as music endures, limiting oneself to a melody of always equal note values is, except in the mastering of a technique, too artificial a device and, as Soderlund tells us, it was "already obsolete in the sixteenth century" (*Direct Approach to Counterpoint*, page vii).

In writing in 16th century style without a C. F., several new resources become possible:

1. Chord changes will be more frequent since there are no given whole notes to limit the choice or duration of triads.

2. The relatively accented passing tone, heretofore encountered after a half note in scalewise descending progression, is now found, still on the third quarter, but in a stream of scalewise descending quarter notes. This idiom usually occurs in approaching a cadence, and the sharp dissonance is all the more pronounced because it is sounded against the preparation of the closing suspension, sometimes even resulting in parallel 7ths or 9ths, as shown in Example 101.

Example 101

[handwritten notes:] 1. struck sus. allowable
2. dis on 3rd beat " if dis is approached contrary motion & stepwise

3. To conform to 16th century usage, time signatures of 4/2 and 3/2 rather than 2/2, are suggested, as shown in the model examples.

4. Imitative beginnings are recommended.

Example 102. FREE WRITING IN TWO PARTS

Example 103

Example 104

Assignment XXVI

Write two short studies in free style in two parts. If the student has difficulty in
getting started, he may, in one of his exercises, copy the opening measures of one
of the model examples and continue it by himself; or he may copy one voice of
one of the models and add a second voice of his own—without further reference to
the model example, of course.

In Three Parts

Nothing needs to be added. Thorough study of the model examples is essential,
and will prove more helpful than many more words would be.

The problem of setting a text is outside the province of this Handbook. Those
interested may consult Jeppesen's already recommended *Counterpoint*, or Soderlund's *Direct Approach to Counterpoint*.

However, if a simple enough text is chosen, such as repeated Alleluias or
Amens, the problem is not difficult, so long as accented syllables are kept on
stronger beats or on rhythmically accented tones, such as long notes or tied notes,
wherever they may fall in the measure. Words could be provided for the model
examples, as is shown in Example 106.

Example 105. FREE WRITING IN THREE PARTS

Example 106

Example 107

Assignment XXVII

Write two free studies in three parts, using imitative entries, and adding a simple text if desired.

CHAPTER 7

Four-Part Writing

First Species in Four Parts

We return to the use of a C. F. for the first lessons in four-part writing.

1. The harmonic basis remains unchanged, but consistent doubling becomes necessary, and incomplete triads will be less frequent.

2. The only doubling not acceptable is that of the leading tone in the final cadence. In the Phrygian mode, this tone is, of course, E.

3. When the C. F. is in an upper voice, an incomplete chord is often unavoidable in the final cadence.

4. In all four-part exercises, the use of all four clefs—treble, alto, tenor, and bass—is required.

Example 108. FIRST SPECIES IN FOUR PARTS

a. *Ionian*

C. F. C   d₆   e₆   F₆   d₆   d   e   d₆   b°₆   C

(Continued)

b. *Dorian transposed*

c. *Phrygian*

Assignment XXVIII

Write exercises in four parts, First Species, to the following C. F., using it in different clefs. Imitative entries must be used at least once.

Fourth Species in Four Parts

It is hardly profitable to write exercises in all species in four parts, since no new principles are involved. However, the managing of suspensions becomes more of a problem as a fourth voice is added. no 2-1

1. Except for the 9–8 and 7–8 suspensions, treated as previously recommended (Rule 2, page 54), and 7–6 accompanied by a 6th (Rule 4, page 68), a note of resolution should not be heard against a suspension.

2. The hardest arrangement to manage is that with Fourth Species in the bass. Accordingly, most of the possibilities of accompanying a suspension and resolution of D to C are shown in Example 109. These may be transposed to other degrees of the mode, sometimes with the help of Musica Ficta, or the three upper voices rearranged, as shown below at "same". Note that the previously excluded $\frac{7}{4}$–$\frac{8}{5}$ suspensions are now acceptable when accompanied by 2–3, as shown at *.

Example 109

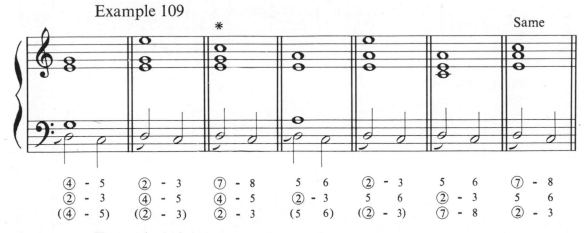

Example 110. FOURTH SPECIES IN FOUR PARTS

a. *Dorian*

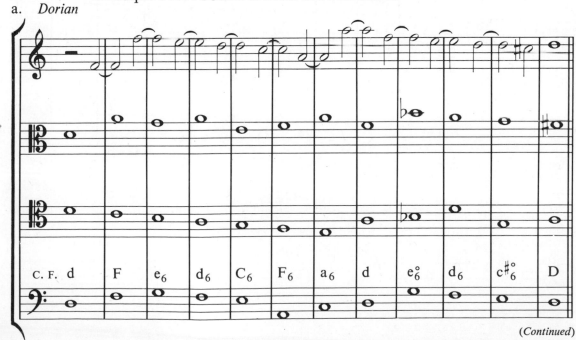

(Continued)

b. *Lydian*

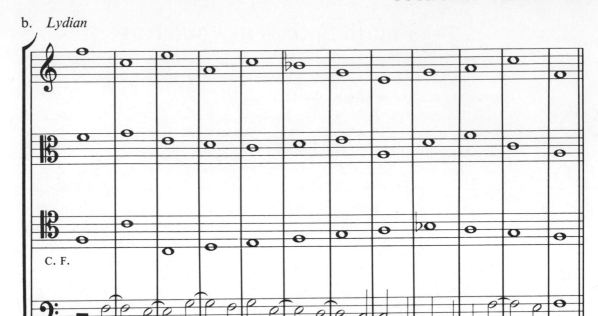

c. *Phrygian transposed*

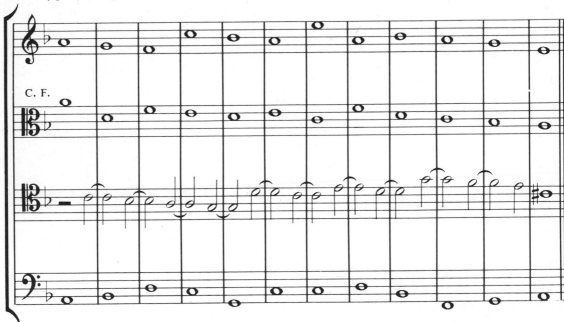

Assignment XXIX

Write two examples of Fourth Species in four parts on the following C. F., using Fourth Species in the bass in one of them.

Combined Species in Four Parts

All combinations of species are possible in four parts, but only a few are profitable for separate study.

1. Combinations of First, Second, and Fourth Species against a C. F. give opportunity for the expression of such suspended discords as:

    a. complete seventh chords
    b. other four-note combinations
    c. incomplete formations used before but now with doublings.

All are illustrated in Example 111, and appropriately labelled.

Example 111

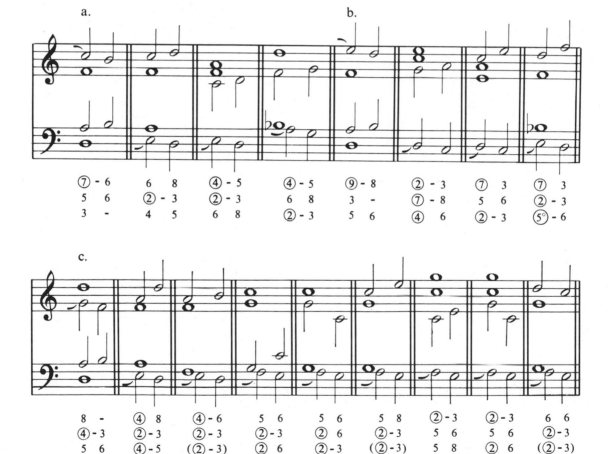

2. Combinations of Second, Third, and Fourth Species give several more interesting suspended discords, notably the complete 6/5/3 chord.

Example 112

⑤°	3	②	3	6	6	6	5	8	3	⑦	3	⑨	3	6	8	④	6	④	6
6	5	④	6	④	6	3	8	⑦	6	8	5	3	5	②	3	②	3	②	3
3	1			②	3	⑤	3	3	1	3	8	5	8	④	6	6	6	6	6

Example 113. COMBINED COUNTERPOINT IN FOUR PARTS—MODEL EXAMPLES

a. *Lydian (First, Second, and Fourth)*

C. F.   F   F₆   C₄⁶ G   a₆   F₆   d₇   b₆°   G₆   a₆   F₆   e₆°   F

b. *Dorian transposed (First, Second, and Fourth)*

C. F.

(Continued)

c. *Aeolian (Second, Third, and Fourth)*

Assignment XXX

Write an example of First, Second, and Fourth Species combined, and another of Second, Third, and Fourth Species combined, on the following C. F.

Fifth Species in Three of Four Parts

The remaining combinations in four voices may be dispensed with, except for the final one with all three voices in Fifth Species. No new principles need be mastered but it should be recalled that all free voices should enter imitatively, either of the C. F. or of each other, with a half note or tied half note after a half rest.

Example 114. FIFTH SPECIES IN THREE OF FOUR PARTS—MODEL EXAMPLES

a. *Phrygian transposed*

(Continued)

b. *Ionian*

c. *Aeolian transposed*

Assignment XXXI

Write examples of Fifth Species in all three counterpoints against the following C. F., used each time in a different voice.

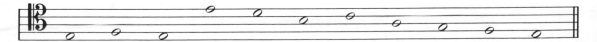

Free Writing in Four Parts

The culmination of this introduction to modal counterpoint is writing in four parts in 16th-century style without C. F.

The opening fragment of the "Benedictus" from Palestrina's *Missa Papae Marcelli* (Example 115) is a suitable close for our *Handbook*. It illustrates several points in technique; but more important, it illustrates the delicate texture and harmonic clarity that characterizes this remarkable Mass. The student now has the means to study it in detail, as well as other masterworks of the Renaissance, and to gain a deeper understanding and appreciation of that literature.

Assignment XXXII

Write an example or two of counterpoint in 16th-century style in four parts, with or without text. Note that in the Palestrina example (Example 115) not all the voices are singing all the time. The rests and fresh entries give animation and variety, both in rhythm and in sonorities.

Example 115. "BENEDICTUS" FROM PALESTRINA'S *Missa Papae Marcelli*

(Continued)

(Continued)

APPENDIXES

Prepared Discords

Prepared Discords in Three-Part Counterpoint

SUSPENSIONS IN UNCOMBINED SPECIES

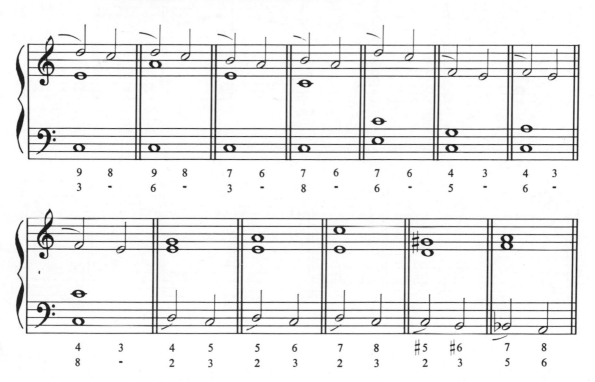

COMBINED SPECIES

Passing Chords

Suspensions

*The parentheses indicate places where a choice of tones is possible.

Double Suspensions

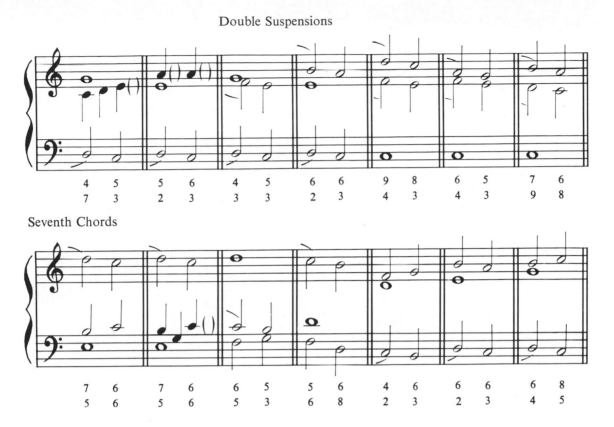

Prepared Discords in Four-Part Counterpoint

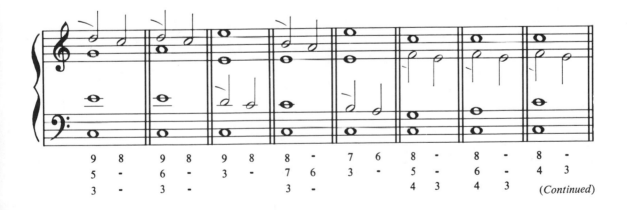

(*Continued*)

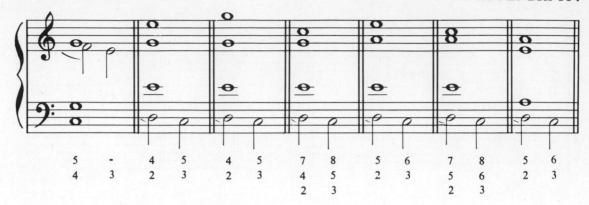

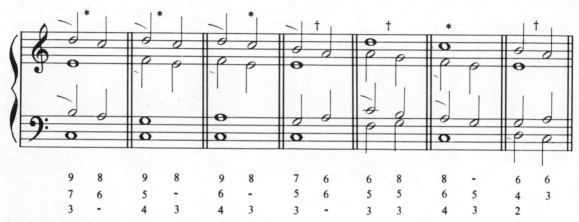

*Double Suspensions
†Seventh Chords

Suggestions for More Advanced Study

As suitable to the student's special interests, modal studies may be continued in composition, comparison of treatises and texts, or in research projects.

Composition

The student will gain artistic insight as well as firm grasp of technique by composing in the sixteenth-century church style, for example, a mass in five or more voices. The books by Jeppesen, Merritt, and Soderlund, named in the Preface, include information on setting Latin texts, as well as discussions of imitation, canon, and fugue, and the over-all treatment of a large work. Translations of selected passages from sixteenth-century treatises in W. O. Strunk's *Source Readings in Music History* reveal the accepted conventions of that era in sacred music. The following single works and collections provide models from the literature:

Palestrina. *Missa Brevis.*
    Missa Papae Marcelli (H. W. Gray edition).
Soderlund, Gustave. *Examples Illustrating the Development of Melodic Line and Contrapuntal Style, From Greek Melody to Mozart* (Rochester, N.Y.: Eastman School of Music, 1932).
————. *Examples of Gregorian Chant and Works of Orlando Lassus, Giovanni Pierluigi Palestrina, and Marco Antonio Ingegneri* (Rochester, N.Y.: Eastman School of Music, 1939).

Comparison of Theoretical Works

A COMPARISON OF FIVE MODERN TREATISES AND TEXTS

The books named below are based on analysis of a great number of sixteenth-century works, most of them selected from the sacred literature.

Jeppesen's *The Style of Palestrina and the Dissonance.*
————. *Counterpoint.*
Merritt's *Sixteenth Century Polyphony.*
Morris' *Contrapuntal Technique in the Sixteenth Century.*
Soderlund's *Direct Approach to Counterpoint in the Sixteenth Century Style.*

The techniques presented by these authors may be compared on the following topics:

Part One: Musical Content

I. Modal scales.
Note whether both Gregorian and polyphonic systems are explained, and whether the Lydian mode is included.

II. Harmonies.
Note especially discussion of the augmented triad, seventh chords, accidentals, free use of the mild dissonances, such as the fourth and diminished fifth, etc.

III. Analysis symbols, if any.

IV. Meter and rhythm.
Note whether harmonic and melodic rhythms are well differentiated.

V. Openings, cadences, and modulations.

VI. Idioms.
Nota Cambiata, The Relatively Accented Passing Tone, the Consonant Fourth, Extended Ornamental Resolutions, etc. are the important items here.

VII. Consecutives.
These must be considered as follows:
In parallel and contrary motion.
In immediate succession and with intervening material.
In the case of fifths, successions of unequal fifths, that is, when one of them is diminished.
In two parts only and in three or more parts.

VIII. Direct octaves and fifths (also called hidden, concealed, or covered).

XI. Melodic leaps and patterns; sequences.

Part Two: Educational Method

I. Use of the Cantus Firmus and Five Species.
Note the author's opinions and his arguments for or against this method. Has he concentrated on the freedom and flexibility of the melodic rhythms and overlooked the regularity of the harmonic rhythms? Has he concentrated on the artistic product and overlooked the educational method by which the composers learned their art?

II. Use of the C clefs.

III. Assignments, if any.

IV. The order in which the material is presented.

V. The author's literary style, organization, etc.

VI. The format of the book, and aids such as index, illustrations, etc.

Part Three: Free Composition

   I. Setting a text in Latin or English.

  II. Explanation of contrapuntal forms and devices.

 III. The form of a large work.

Part Four: Summary

   I. Strong points, as a text, or as a treatise, or both.

  II. Weak points, as above.

 III. Distinctive features, such as historical background, explanation of the notation, treatment of secular music, etc.

A COMPARISON OF TWO CLASSIC TREATISES AND TEXTS

Fux, Johann Joseph. *Steps to Parnassus* (*Gradus ad Parnassum*) 1725. Trans. A. Mann (New York: 1943).
Morley, Thomas. *A Plain and Easy Introduction to Practical Music*, 1597. Alec Harman, ed. (New York: n.d.) "The Second Part" only, for this comparison.

Research Projects

    A few bibliographical references are provided to help the student begin his research. General reference works, named below, are given in shortened form under the topic heads:

Grove's Dictionary of Music and Musicians, 5th ed. (London, 1954).
The New Oxford History of Music (London, 1957-   ).
The Oxford History of Music (Oxford, 1901).
Source Readings in Music History. W. O. Strunk, ed. (New York: 1950).

THE MODES AS SCALE-BASIS FOR MONOPHONIC AND POLYPHONIC SONG

Apel, Willi. *Gregorian Chant* (Bloomington, Ind.: 1959).
Grove's. "Modes," Vol. V, 797; "Polyphony," Vol. VI, 849.
New Oxford History. "Medieval Song," Vol. 2, 220; Modes, Vol. 2, 110, 123, 232.
Oxford History. Vol. 1, 45.
Reese, Gustave. *Music in the Middle Ages* (New York: 1940).
———. *Music in the Renaissance* (New York: 1950).
Riemann, Hugo. *History of Music Theory*, Book II. Trans. Raymond Haggh (University of Nebraska Press, 1962).

    See also passages in books by Jeppesen, Merritt, and Soderlund, named in the Preface.

METER, RHYTHM, AND TEMPO IN SIXTEENTH-CENTURY MUSIC

Apel, Willi. *The Notation of Polyphonic Music* (New York: 1945).
———. *Harvard Dictionary of Music*, 452.
Grove's. Vol. VI, 853.

Morley, Thomas. *A Plain and Easy Introduction to Practical Music*, "The First Part."
Sachs, Curt. *Rhythm and Tempo* (New York: 1953).
Reese, Gustave. *Music in the Renaissance* (New York: 1954).

See also passages in books by Jeppesen, Morris, and Soderlund.

THE GREAT THEORISTS OF THE RENAISSANCE

Grove's. Articles on Zarlino, Zacconi, Morley, etc.
Jeppesen. *Counterpoint*, essay on the history of contrapuntal theory.
Source Readings. Translations of writings by sixteenth-century theorists.

THE NOTATION OF RENAISSANCE MUSIC

Apel, Willi. *The Notation of Polyphonic Music* (New York: 1945).
The New Oxford History. Vol. II, 12.

IMPROVISED ORNAMENTATION

Ferand, E. T. *Anthology of Music: Improvisation in Nine Centuries of Western Music* (New York: 1961).
Morley, Thomas. *A Plain and Easy Introduction to Practical Music*, 140 and following.

THE ENGLISH SCHOOL

Fellowes, Edmund H. *English Cathedral Music* (London: 1941).
————. *The English Madrigal School* (London: Stainer, n.d.).

EXPRESSING THE VERBAL TEXT

Index

DATE DUE